PAINTING PICTURES, CHANGING LIVES

SOME PARABLES AND MIRACLES OF JESUS

GEORGE MITCHELL

This book is dedicated to the staff and students of Scott Theological College, Machakos, Kenya, and all my African brothers and sisters.

This book arose from a series of broadcast talks given on Revival FM, a local Christian radio station in Cumbernauld, near Glasgow.
This explains the conversational, rather than academic style, hopefully for people of faith, and people of no faith. I have edited the scripts, and included the Biblical text of the parables and miracles. I have also included questions for discussion, which may be helpful for group study and discussion.

I am grateful to my colleagues at Revival FM, especially Dorian Stone, for their help in the studio, and for the Directors, who have encouraged me to go into print.

As always, I am deeply grateful to the library staff at International Christian College, especially Lucy, Gudrun and Anna, and to all the staff, especially Kenneth and Jim at Kenwil Print and Design, the printers, for all their help.

ABOUT THE AUTHOR

George Mitchell was born and raised in Glasgow, Scotland, and was converted and trained for Christian service at Lambhill Evangelical Church, and London Bible College (now London School of Theology).

George spent five years as a metallurgist in the steel industry, seventeen years as a full-time teacher and lecturer, and over twenty years as a Baptist pastor in Scotland. He is a guest lecturer at the International Christian College, Glasgow, and Scott Theological College, Machakos, Kenya.

George enjoys football, badminton, golf and trumpet-playing. George and Jean have been married since 1964, and have a son Finlay who is married to Fiona, and a daughter Janet, who is married to Billy. They have two grandchildren, Kirstin and Angus.

George has had five books published – 'Comfy Glasgow', a personal testimony, 'Chained and Cheerful', a commentary on Philippians, 'Revival Man', the story of Jock Troup, revivalist-evangelist, 'Prisoner for Christ', a biography of John Bunyan for young people, and 'Born Free', studies in Galatians.

PAINTING PICTURES, CHANGING LIVES
SOME PARABLES AND MIRACLES OF JESUS

CHAPTER HEADINGS.

The Biblical text reproduced is the New International Version.

SOURCES.

T Adeyemo, ed. Africa Bible Commentary, Zondervan, Word Alive, Nairobi. 2006

JM Boice. The Parables of Jesus. Moody Press, Chicago. 1983

W. Barclay. New Testament Words. SCM Press, London. 1983

C Brown, ed. The New International Dictionary of New Testament Theology, vol 2. Paternoster, Exeter. 1976

JD Douglas, ed. The Illustrated Bible Dictionary, vols 1-3. Inter-Varsity Press, Tyndale House, Leicester. 1988

G Duncan. Preach the Word. Marshall Pickering, London. 1989

JB Green, S McKnight, IH Marshall, eds. Dictionary of Jesus and the Gospels. Inter-Varsity Press, Leicester. 1992

D Guthrie. New Testament Introduction. Tyndale Press, London. 1965

D Guthrie. New Testament Theology. Inter-Varsity Press, Leicester. 1981

J Hultgren. The Parables of Jesus. WB Eerdmans, Grand Rapids, Michigan. 2000

AM Hunter. Interpreting the Parables. SCM Press, London. 1981

J Jeremias. The Parables of Jesus. SCM Press, London 1963

H Lockyer. All the Parables of the Bible. Pickering and Inglis, London. 1970

RP Martin. New Testament Foundations. Vol 1: The Four Gospels. Paternoster, Exeter. 1975

GC Morgan. Studies in the Four Gospels. Fleming H Revell, Westwood, New Jersey. 1931

GC Morgan. The Parables and Metaphors of our Lord. Marshall, Morgan and Scott, London 1944

CC Ryrie. The Miracles of our Lord. Loizeaux Brothers, Neptune, New Jersey. 1988

J Stalker. The Life and Teaching of our Lord. AMG Publishers. 1995

RH Stein. Jesus the Messiah. Inter-Varsity Press, Leicester. 1996

MC Tenney. New Testament Survey, Revised by WM Dunnett. Inter-Varsity Press, Leicester. 1977

V Verbrugge, ed. The NIV Theological Dictionary of New Testament Words. Zondervan, Grand Rapids, Michigan. 2000

WE Vine. Expository Dictionary of New Testament Words. Macdonald Publishing, McLean, Virginia

Keith Warrington. Jesus the Healer. Paternoster Press, Carlisle. 2000

David Wenham. The Parables of Jesus. Hodder and Stoughton, London 1989

M Zerwick and M Grosvenor. A Grammatical Analysis of the Greek New Testament. Editrice Pontifico, Instituto Biblico, Rome. 1993

CHAPTER ONE

THE BIBLE AND THE PARABLES

Welcome to the first part of this book, which looks at the role of the Bible in society, before we consider some of the parables and miracles of the Lord Jesus Christ.

The Bible has had a profound effect on people's lives. The word 'Bible' means 'the books' – the Bible is really a mini-library of sixty-six books, written by over thirty authors over at least a thirteen-hundred-year period. There have been times when well-meaning special groups, like church leaders or academics, have tried to shield the Bible from the people, by keeping it in an unfamiliar language, like Latin, or by saying that ordinary people did not have the technical know-how to understand its contents. In sixteenth-century England, William Tyndale, a graduate of Oxford and Cambridge, was so appalled at the clergy's ignorance of the Bible, that he set about making a translation from the Hebrew and Greek original manuscripts of the Old and New Testaments into English. He is said to have told a priest: 'If God spare my life, ere many years pass, I will cause a boy that driveth the plough to know more of the Scriptures (ie the Bible) than thou dost.'

This prophecy of Tyndale was fulfilled, in the life of John Brown, a sixteen-year-old shepherd boy from the hills of Abernethy in Perthshire, Scotland. The year was 1738, and the place was Alexander McCulloch's bookshop in St Andrews. The lad walked into the shop, and asked for a Greek New Testament. 'Boy!' exclaimed the Professor of Greek who happened to be in the shop at that moment, 'if you can read that book, you shall have it for nothing!' Soon a fine leather volume was in the lad's hand, and to the amazement of all present, he read a section, and won his prize...

By the afternoon, John Brown the shepherd lad was back among his flock on the hills. He had walked some forty-eight miles since the previous evening to obtain his treasure. To see the far-flung consequences of Tyndale's prophecy and John Brown's fulfilment, we have to speed on seventy years, to the 6th of February 1806. John Brown of Abernethy had become one of the most famous of Scottish preachers, as minister for 36 years at Haddington, East Lothian, for twenty years of those as Divinity Professor, and now his grandson was being ordained in 1806 as minister of the Secession Church at Biggar. The Bible had a telling effect on the Brown family.

We now travel in time, back to a man who wrote the first-ever Christian autobiography. His story is that of a profligate son with a tortured soul, and a godly mother who never gave up on him. He could have been a contender for a series in any scandal-sheet newspaper. In his 'Confessions', he tells us something about his background. Augustine was born in the area we know as Algeria, Africa, in AD 354, to a pagan father and a devout Christian mother, called Monica. After an account of a childhood in which he robbed pantries and orchards, he became a teacher of rhetoric in Carthage, North Africa, and as a young man he co-habited with a girl he could not marry because she was below his status in society. She had a baby to him, little Adeodatus ('gift of

God'). Augustine went through mental turmoil, which was made worse by his joining a sect called the Manichaeans, who condemned having sexual relations, and regarded it as a crime to have babies, which they reckoned was imprisoning new souls in sinful bodies. He travelled from Carthage to Rome, and then to Milan. After putting away his girl-friend, Augustine was promised to another girl two years too young to marry, and while he was waiting for her to come of age, he took another partner! Some of today's young people talk about sex as if they invented it, but Augustine seemed to have cornered a fair slice of that market about eighteen hundred years ago!

Augustine began admiring the Christian monks of Egypt for being able to control their emotions and passions, and later came under the spell of Bishop Ambrose of Milan, a magnificent preacher, who directed him to the New Testament. Augustine was in great torment. Bemoaning his fate as sinner, and literally tearing his hair out, one day while he was in the garden, he heard the voice of a child, crooning 'tolle lege, tolle lege', which means 'take up and read, take up and read'. He happened to open the New Testament at the apostle Paul's Letter to the Romans, chapter 13 where it says: 'We can't afford to waste a minute, must not squander these precious daylight hours in frivolity and sleeping around and dissipation, in bickering and grabbing everything in sight. Get out of bed and get dressed! Don't loiter and linger, waiting until the very last minute. Dress yourselves in Christ, and be up and about.' (the Message Translation). The rest, as they say, is history. Augustine found peace with God, and was reunited with his family. He became Bishop of Hippo in North Africa, and became one of the greatest leaders of the Early Church.

What does the Bible say about itself? In the Second Letter of Peter, the writer describes the Bible authors like this: 'men they were, but driven along by the Holy Spirit, they wrote the words of God.' The writers retained their individuality, their personal quirks and writing styles. The God who inspired them did not employ clones, robots or dictating machines. The verb translated 'driven' is used in the Book of Acts of the wind driving Paul's ship in a storm. What they wrote has the authentic tang of the divine about it. In Paul's second Letter to Timothy, we read that 'all Scripture is God-breathed...' (2 Timothy 3 verse 16), either breathed out by God (expiration), or breathed into by God (inspiration). I prefer to accept the second option, because it parallels the idea early in Genesis (chapter 2 verse 7) of God making mankind from the dust of the earth, and 'breathing into man's nostrils the breath of life'. The Bible is an inspired book. Professor Jim Packer draws a helpful comparison between the nature of Scripture and the nature of Christ. He says that both Scripture and Christ reflect the idea of a perfect blend or combination of the human and the divine.

In his introduction to his translation/paraphrase of the New Testament, JB Phillips describes the tingling effect that Scripture had on him. He compares his job as a translator to that of an electrician who has been sent to rewire an old house which has been lying unoccupied for ages, with the power switched off. Imagine his surprise to find that there was power surging through the wires! – enough to make his hair stand on end... He said that as he worked on it, the Bible seemed as alive as it had ever been, and his job was merely to fit new conduit for the wires. The Bible is alive!

A printer was producing a slim-line edition of the New Testament, but couldn't fit these words to put them on the spine of his edition, and decided to print 'New TNT', in other words this book is dynamite!

In the 1980s I was in the hall of Adelaide Place Baptist Church, Bath Street, Glasgow, training counsellors for a mission led by an Argentinian preacher Luis Palau. One of the exercises was to arrange chairs in groups of six, so that the counsellors-to-be could share their experiences of God. I had to go round the groups, and 'catch the flavour' of what they were saying. My attention was riveted by one young Glasgow lad's story. He was a burglar by trade, and after some time became troubled as he thought of the sadness and the sense of violation his activities brought to the householders whose homes he had burgled, particularly elderly people. He then told how he started, in his free time (I have no idea when a burglar's free time would be), to read his mother's Gideon Bible. As he read the Bible, he said he felt increasingly unclean, and when he read the story of Christ's limitless love shown by his dying on the Cross, he prayed for God's forgiveness, and stopped being a burglar. His life was totally changed. This all happened without any human help, apart from using his mother's Bible.

GM Trevelyan the secular historian argued strongly that the Bible-inspired revival in Britain under the preaching of John Wesley and George Whitefield in the eighteenth century saved our country from the kind of blood-bath France experienced during the Terror which preceded Napoleon's rise to power.

Now we can turn from consideration of the Bible's effects on people and society to consider some of the parables and miracle stories contained in it.

The title of this book gives clues about the approach which will be adopted. The **miracles** section of the title is related mainly to healing miracles, but the chapter dealing with the feeding of the crowd on the hill, must have had life-changing effects on everyone present that day, including Jesus' disciples, so the title remains valid. The first part of the title is also valid, because **parables** are word pictures. There is an old Arab proverb 'he is the best teacher who can turn the ear into an eye.' Visualisation was certainly a key component in the teaching of Jesus, who was the greatest teacher who ever lived. The title 'Rabbi' is a Hebrew/Aramaic title, meaning 'my Great One' (the term 'Rabboni' is a diminutive form of endearment, meaning 'my Dear Great One'). Luke, who arguably wrote mainly for non-Jews, omits the term, and alongside the other Gospels, uses the term 'didaskalos' usually in the vocative form of address 'didaskale' – 'Teacher'. In the Gospels, Jesus speaks of Himself in the third person as didaskalos (Matthew 26 verse 18. Mark 14 verse 14. John 13 verses 13 and 14). However He is addressed, the verdict of the temple guards stands the test of time: 'No-one ever spoke the way this man does.'

Parables had been used in Judaism from at least the time of David. The prophet Nathan's parable of the ewe lamb was used by the Lord to convict King David of his sin of adultery with Bathsheba around 950BC (see 2 Samuel chapters 12 and 13). Fiebig and Feldmann have identified about 2000 rabbinic parables. Of course, Jesus is recognised as the Master Teacher of parables. A parable is literally 'a thrown alongside thing' (para-bole), a comparison or an analogy. The schoolboy howler is a useful anti-definition; 'A parable is a heavenly story with no earthly meaning'. In fact, a parable is a story about earthly things containing spiritual truth as an integral component of the story. It may be compared to a railway track, with two lines of truth running parallel to each other. KR Snodgrass wrote: 'parables are imaginary gardens with real toads in them.' Parables contain simile elements: 'the kingdom of heaven is **like** a mustard seed..' , where a comparison is made, and metaphor elements 'the seed **is** the word..', where a direct identification is made.

Parables take up a significant part, about one-third, of the teaching of Jesus. The scatter would be about 16% of Mark, and about 43% of the special Matthew source M, and about 52% of the special Luke source.
This is a distinctive feature of Jesus' teaching. Jewish rabbis used parables occasionally, but Jesus, especially in addressing the crowds, spoke pictorially most of the time.

We should be aware of the phenomenon of the story-teller in a non-literate society, and of the place of memory training in a culture where oral teaching occupied centre stage. The world in which Jesus lived was a world without the means of communication like radio or television, newspapers, word processors, or DVDs. The story-teller was part newscaster, part archivist and part entertainer, a vital part of the fabric of the ancient world. He was physically the centre of attraction. He would know local history and local scandal, and would lead the people verbally from the familiar to the unfamiliar.
AM Hunter finds about 60 parables in the Gospels, and disagrees with scholars who say that John's Gospel has allegories and is parable-free. He cites the Woman in Travail John 16 verse 21, the Traveller at Sunset, John 12 verse 35 following, and sees a parable embedded in John chapter 10 verses 1-5.
AM Hunter claims that five parables teach truth by direct example rather than allegory. These are the Pharisee and the Publican, Dives and Lazarus, the Rich Fool, the Good Samaritan, and the Sheep and the Goats.

Some scholars have tried to separate the elements in parables which distinguish them from allegories. In an allegory, each detail of the story has its counterpart in the network of meaning. Parables contain life-like features – loaves are loaves, and stones are stones, but allegories need not be life-like.

Parables slip easily into the sleeve of teaching and story-telling, generally. We move from the known to the unknown, and from the familiar to the unfamiliar. They combine the Eastern mind's innate love of pictorial speech with everyone's love of a good story. General similitudes deal with familiar truths or processes held in common in the Hebrew 'mashal' or proverb. The proverb is not presenting what men commonly do, covered by verbs in the present tense. The parable tells what one man did, using several past tenses: 'See! A sower went out to sow.'

I sometimes find a comparison between comedy and parabolic teaching. We distil the details of a joke, retaining the most important points, and the boiled-down form encapsulates the funny element. In the actual telling, there is an element of repetition in the build-up to what is called 'the punch line'. Another feature of story-telling is the 'rule of contrast' between rich and poor, virtue and vice, wisdom and folly. Sometimes the 'rule of three' pertains to the telling – 'there was an Englishman, an Irishman, and a Scotsman..' In Jesus' parables, we have the three travellers in the story of the Good Samaritan, or the three excuse-makers in the parable of the Great Supper. Another feature of the joke or parabolic style is the 'rule of end stress', where there is repetition as the story proceeds, but emphasis comes in the last element of the series. For example, there is a build-up to the sending of the son in the parable of the Vineyard, or the final element in the parable of the Talents.

Jesus used parables as a teaching tool to sift His hearers. There were those who flocked to hear Him, particularly in the 'year of public favour' during His ministry in Galilee, who just wanted to enjoy a good story. But there were others who came to Jesus because they were on a spiritual search for God. Parables sorted out the hearers and rung bells with a few as they thought about what they had heard. There is a hint of hidden truth in the face-value of Mark 4 verse 11 following, as if Jesus meant to confuse His audience, but the parables are not there like conundrums to confuse or obscure, so the face-value interpretation cannot be the real one. He constantly encouraged His audiences to think deeply; 'he who has ears to hear, let him hear' was a stock phrase. Those who were earnestly seeking God would find Him.

There is **a danger element** in parables, both for the hearer and the speaker. The parables of Jesus are like verbal commandos setting explosives, producing delayed-action responses. They make the hearer lower his guard, and he is left defenceless, when the aftermath of the teaching hits him. AM Hunter quotes PG Wodehouse, who puts a description of a parable in the mouth of one of his characters. The parable seems at first a pleasant yarn, but keeps something up its sleeve, which pops up and leaves you flat! The element of risk for the storyteller was clear in the Nathan incident in 2 Samuel chapters 12 and 13. Nathan was using the story form as he faced the king with his sin, and his head could be off as a result! In the case of Jesus, the parable of the Wicked Vinedressers proved to be the straw which broke the camel's back with the contemporary religious leaders. 'When the chief priests and the Pharisees heard Jesus' parables, they knew He was talking about them. They looked for a way to arrest Him, but they were afraid of the crowd, because the people held that He was a prophet.'

With these few words, let's proceed to become involved with a few parables.

QUESTIONS.

1. How do you think the Bible has affected Scotland?

2. Discuss any family or personal connections you have with the Bible

3. Are there ways the Bible has affected British culture without people being aware of it? Discuss.

4. What does it mean to say 'the Bible is an inspired book.' ?

5. How would you respond to someone who says 'I am a private Christian. I just need my Bible. I don't need church.'?

6. What is a parable?   Define and discuss.

7. How important are the parables in the teaching of Jesus?

8. What was special or distinctive about how Jesus used parables?

CHAPTER TWO

THE PARABLE OF THE SOWER.   Matthew chapter 13 verses 3-9, 18-23

Then He told them many things in parables, saying:
'A farmer went out to sow his seed. As he was scattering the seed, some fell along the path, and the birds came and ate it up. Some fell on rocky places, where it did not have much soil. It sprang up quickly, because the soil was shallow. But when the sun came up, the plants were scorched, and they withered because they had no root. Other seed fell among thorns, which grew up and choked the plants. Still other seed fell on good soil, where it produced a crop - a hundred, sixty or thirty times what was sown. He who has ears, let him hear...'

'Listen then to what the parable of the sower means: when anyone hears the message about the kingdom, and does not understand it, the evil one comes and snatches away what was sown in his heart. This is the seed sown along the path. The one who received the seed that fell on rocky places is the man who hears the word and at once receives it with joy. But since he has no root, he lasts only a short time. When trouble or persecution come because of the word, he quickly falls away. The one who received the seed that fell among the thorns is the man who hears the word, but the worries and cares of life and the deceitfulness of wealth choke it, making it unfruitful. But the one who received the seed that fell on good soil is the man who hears the word and understands it. He produces a crop, yielding a hundred, sixty, or thirty times what was sown.'

PARABLE OF THE SOWER

In the opening chapter, we looked at some of the characteristics of parables, and attempted some sort of definition. It is now time to look at the central character of the Bible – the Lord Jesus Christ – and His teaching in the parables.

Jesus had some considerable barriers to overcome to establish His credibility as a teacher:

First of all, he was **young**, in an ageist, stratified, hidebound Jewish context. He was about thirty when He quit the carpenter's workshop to become a travelling Rabbi, or Teacher. Not nearly experienced enough, they would reckon.

Secondly, He was a **Northerner**, a 'hick from the hills' of Galilee in the north of Israel, with a northern accent or dialect. This would have a jarring effect on the posh-speaking 'smoothies' of Jerusalem.

Thirdly, He came from **Nazareth**, a 'you've got to be kidding' kind of town, which didn't even get a mention in lists ancient or modern. Nazareth isn't mentioned in the Book of Joshua's list of the conquered towns of Northern Israel, nor in the list of Northern towns drawn up by the Jewish historian Josephus.

Fourthly, **He had never studied with the top Rabbis in Jerusalem**. Although Luke's Gospel describes a cameo incident when the twelve-year old Jesus was visiting Jerusalem at the time of the Passover Festival, and was listening and asking the scholars questions, He was never formally trained by them.

Finally, **He did not follow their approved teaching style**, which was to show off your erudition to students or commoners by quoting from a long tradition of scholarly authorities. The resulting teaching was what some might call deep, and others might call 'muddy'. Jesus in some ways a unique Teacher, but in other directions great teachers have followed His style. Jesus' teaching style was to make the truths He taught simple, clear and visual to his hearers, and the impact of it was that while He did not quote the authorities, **He spoke with authority.** That really stuck in the throats of Jewish academics, and generated a fair amount of 'customer resistance' among them.

To help us to understand the parables, we have to understand the role of the story-teller in ancient society. He was the man in the know about local family affairs and history. His tales would be the distillation of familiar and unfamiliar facts.

The Bible books were written, and the teaching of Jesus was given, in an essentially agricultural context – sowing and reaping, planting and ploughing, growing crops, farmers and barns, and donkeys falling into ditches. The stuff of His teaching involved the everyday stories of country folk – wayward sons, patched clothes, primitive lighting, one-roomed cottages, lost sheep and mother hens and their chickens. Now there were those who came to hear Jesus, who were greatly impressed by His down-to-earth approach and His lively presentation, who filtered out any reference to God, and went away glad or contented. The four Good News stories, the Gospels, quote Jesus frequently as saying: 'He who has ears to hear, let him hear', which probably was not meant as an insult to the hard-of-hearing, but a call to listen carefully and search tirelessly for the spiritual truth behind the parables. In other words , the parables were a teaching tool used by Jesus to sort out, or sift, His hearers into those who came with a superficial interest in the entertainment of storytelling, and those with a heart-hunger to find God behind the teaching of Jesus. I suppose that it could be much the same today, and some folk are quite unmoved and unimpressed by Christian truth.

At Easter, we can watch Robert Powell star in Zeffereli's film of the Life of Jesus, or Mel Gibson's 'The Passion of the Christ', and turn our chairs round and tuck into a chicken tikka masala as if nothing had happened. Occasionally, folk will tell us how they were moved or changed by such spectacles, but they are the exception. Yet perhaps the old hymn-writer was correct:

> 'Deep in the human heart, crushed by the tempter
> Feelings lie buried which grace can restore,
> Touched by a loving hand, wakened by kindness
> Chords that were broken will vibrate once more.'

There are many people who don't have much time for the institutional church as it is today. I don't blame them. Sleaze tends to stick, and people become disillusioned at the strange goings-on of some Christians. Some of the tele-evangelists get the majority of real Christians a bad name. It has been my experience that people who reject the church retain a respect for the Person of Jesus, and the teaching of Jesus. We don't give up using money because there is counterfeit about! The existence of counterfeit reminds us that the real thing must be worth copying! Also, the Bank recognises counterfeit when it crops up...Similarly, the parables of Jesus have an authentic ring about them, and help us at the lowest level to admire truth displayed by the Master Teacher. It is helpful to look at the distinctive differences between parables.

Looking at life through the teaching of Jesus in His parables, we've noticed that **simplicity, clarity** and **visualisation** were important teaching tools for Jesus. **Repetition** was also important. When we read about Jesus the Rabbi, or didaskalos (which means 'Teacher') in the Gospels, we find that some of the parables are repeated in different social or time settings. It wasn't simply a varied importation of the slightly varied stories into the Gospels.

The best explanation for the differences in background is that He deliberately repeated His teaching on different occasions and at different times. Preachers have been known to repeat sermons, or soloists have repeated items from their repertoire. When I was a schoolboy, I remember the contrast between two French teachers I had. One was a very prim lady (the Scottish word would be 'perjink'), who recorded all her teaching and all our misdeeds in a notebook, and was shocked if you forgot something which she had noted down she had taught you on the 23 September! The other teacher was a devil-may-care, chain-smoking ex-despatch rider from World War II, who thought that if he told you something a million times, you **might** be able to remember it. Repetition was one of his secrets, as it was with Jesus.

The Gospels contain about 50 or 60 parables, and about 20 mini-parables, which the technocrats call 'parabolic illustrations'. Scholars vary in their classification. Some of Jesus' parables teach one main lesson. For example, the Parable of the Good Samaritan is meant to provide the answer to a specific question Jesus was asked....'Who is my neighbour?' To answer this question, Jesus told a story about a man who was mugged, and left to bleed to death. The wounded man was ignored or passed by at different times, when two representative religious leaders saw him lying isolated and bleeding on that bandit-infested road. A Samaritan, who should have been his hated enemy, stopped and gave on the spot first-aid, then carried him on his donkey to an inn, where he paid the inn-keeper for his continuing care. It becomes ridiculous when, as some people used to do, each detail in the story is given a spiritual meaning, and a parable becomes a happy hunting-ground for truth, where the prizes go to the most ingenious.
The real answer Jesus gave is that my neighbour is the person in need who comes across my path in life. How's that for truth that never goes out of date!

A few of Jesus' parables teach a variety, or range of truths. We can be sure of this, because when Jesus told the parable of the Sower, He provided a key to its interpretation which gives spiritual weight to each detail of the story. The parable of the Sower fits into the category 'Parables of the Kingdom', that is, parables about God's kingly rule in the lives of individuals and society.

The parable of the Sower centred on the varying 'reception areas' for the farmer's seed, and the results they produced. As Jesus told the parable, it is perfectly feasible that there was a farmer, or sower at work before their very eyes. The work becomes personalised in the farmer sowing the seed. Jesus in His teaching classifies four kinds of soil – the road, the gravelly or stony ground, the weeds, and the good earth. Each growing medium yields or produces different results, some productive, and some not productive.

In Jesus' parable of the Sower, or the Farmer, the seed which fell on the road illustrates the difference between hearing and listening to God's Good News of Jesus Christ. Teachers are always saying to classes : 'You can hear me, but are you listening to me?' It also highlights the difference between reception of a vital message and the responsibility to respond to it. The Evil One characterised here exercises a devilish force in snatching away the message like the birds snatched away the seed.

The gravel, or stony medium gives the impression of an initial surge of enthusiasm in response to receiving the message. However, the flashy beginning is only short-lived, and the message becomes non-productive, like the seed in shallow earth wilting before the heat of the sun. Opinion varies as to whether the stony ground is better understood as a shallow layer of earth with a stony table beneath it, or ground containing many stones.

The seed choked with thorns illustrates a life where the message is received, and is initially productive but is subsequently choked out by what the New English Bible calls 'the cares of this life, and the false glamour of riches'. When we think about it, the relevance and freshness of Jesus' teaching comes home to us. There are people who are bowed down with care and taken in by the cut-throat rat race for status and things. Sometimes the care is self-generated, because of poor relationships or thoughtless words, or carelessness with money, or a refusal to share our load with others. It's also so easy to get sucked into the swamp of false thinking that pleasure is in direct proportion to how much you spent to get it. It is all too easy to forget or choose to ignore the spiritual dimension of life. The Good News that God loves us and Christ died for us seems to have no impact any longer.

The seed which fell on good ground illustrates someone who has grasped God's truth from day one, and the seed has been nourishing and growing in that person's life ever since. They have become happy and fulfilled, and a source of joy and encouragement to others.

Parables are our flexible friends. The principles in them are timeless, and the details of the stories can be transplanted into any culture. The farmer could be a sales rep leaving samples, the vineyard-keeper could be a master-tailor leaving samples of patterns, and so on. Since in this parable, Jesus says the seed is the news of the kingdom, we'll stick to the primary idea that it means the message of God's rule in the hearts of individuals or society. The News is like the sunshine of God's Word shining in our hearts.

Bishop Taylor Smith said the message of the Bible could be summarised in three phrases: God is, God is Love, and God Loves Me. Now, the same sun which softens and melts the wax, hardens the clay, so the message can have varying effects on people's lives. A child can hear the message, and it can be snatched away by some cynical friend. Some youth who was initially interested in the Christian message might discover that the person who first shared it with him was an 'idol with feet of clay', whose walk does not match his talk, so to speak, so the young person loses interest. Somebody in their twenties or thirties might become too absorbed in making a living, or too taken up with 'having a life' to give their lives to God. A calloused heart or closed mind and ears may cause their spiritual lives to become unfruitful. The great encouraging factors in the parable of the Sower are the possibility of change and the certainty of harvest for those whose lives are impressionable and available when God's message strikes home.

Jim Elliott was a champion wrestler at Wheaton College Illinois in the 1940s. His personal journal expresses his desire to 'live to the hilt every situation you believe to be the will of God'. This included marrying Elisabeth Howard in 1953, and working hard to reach the Stone-Age tribe, the Auca Indians of Ecuador in South America with the message of God's love. Two of his famous sayings were: 'Wherever you are, be ALL there', and 'He is no fool who gives what he cannot keep to gain what he cannot lose.' He knew the risks involved, and coolly faced the possibility of martyrdom. He died aged 28, with four other friends , killed by an Auca Indian's lance on a sandbank in the

Curaray River in Ecuador. His life and martyrdom has inspired and challenged countless others, as the seed produced a harvest beyond his wildest dreams.

In the next chapter, we'll look at life through Jesus' parable about a dysfunctional family....

QUESTIONS

1. What does the term 'Rabbi' mean? What does he do?

2. Give FIVE reasons why Jesus was unacceptable to official Judaism as a Rabbi.

3. List FOUR teaching skills Jesus used as a Rabbi. Are they still relevant in modern teaching? Discuss

4. Jesus told a parable about a Good Samaritan. Why did the Jews despise the Samaritans? Discuss. Why was the Samaritan's intervention unusual?

5. What were the FOUR 'reception areas' for the seed in the parable of the Sower?

6. Discuss examples of singles and multiple truths taught in parables. Into which category do you fit the parable of the Sower?

7. What explanation did Jesus give of the meaning of the parable of the Sower? (Matthew 13 verses 19-23). Discuss any modern equivalents of the four kinds of ground.

8. What application, if any, does this parable have in relation to the Church's evangelism?

CHAPTER 3

THE PARABLE OF THE PRODIGAL SON. Luke 15 verses 11-32

'Jesus continued: 'There was a man who had two sons. The younger one said to his father, 'Father, give me my share of the estate..' So he divided his property between them. Not long after that, the younger son got together all he had, set off for a distant country and there squandered his wealth in wild living. After he had spent everything, there was a severe famine in that whole country, and he began to be in need. So he went and hired himself out to a citizen of that country, who sent him to his fields to feed pigs. He longed to fill his stomach with the pods that the pigs were eating, but no-one gave him anything.

When he came to his senses, he said, 'How many of my father's hired men have food to spare, and here I am starving to death! I will set out and go back to my father and say to him: 'Father I have sinned against you. I am no longer worthy to be called your son; make me like one of your hired men.' But while he was still a long way off, his father saw him and was filled with compassion for him; he ran to his son, threw his arms around him and kissed him. The son said to him: 'Father, I have sinned against heaven and against you. I am no longer worthy to be called your son.'

But the father said to his servants, 'Quick! Bring the best robe and put it on him. Put a ring on his finger and sandals on his feet. Bring the fattened calf and kill it. Let's have a feast and celebrate. For this son of mine was dead and is alive again; he was lost and is found.' So they began to celebrate.

Meanwhile, the older son was in the field. When he came near the house, he heard music and dancing. So he called one of the servants and asked him what was going on. 'Your brother has come,' he replied, 'and your father has killed the fattened calf because he has him back safe and sound.'

The older brother became angry and refused to go in. So his father went out and pleaded with him. But he answered his father, 'Look! All these years I've been slaving for you and never disobeyed your orders. Yet you never even gave me a young goat so I could celebrate with my friends. But when this son of yours who has squandered your property with prostitutes comes home, you kill the fattened calf for him!'
'My son,' the father said, 'you are always with me, and everything I have is yours. But we had to celebrate and be glad, because this brother of yours was dead and is alive again; he was lost and is found.'

THE PARABLE OF THE PRODIGAL SON

The Parables of Jesus have a timeless quality about them. Their cultural relevance extend not only to the New Testament period, but to our own time. Just think of the titles that could be given to the story we're considering in this chapter. The traditional title for it was 'The Parable of the Prodigal Son', but it has also been called 'The Parable of the Compassionate Father', 'The Parable of the Dysfunctional Family', or 'The Parable of the Lost Sons', which links it to the other two parables in Luke's Gospel, chapter 15 about the Lost Sheep, and the Lost Coin. An African commentator calls it 'The Parable of the Waiting, Running, Embracing God'. Another scholar calls it 'The Parable of the Two Young Wasters'.

Earlier, we saw that a parable is a story about everyday life, with spiritual overtones. Jesus, like lots of teachers before Him, used parables (scholars have identified at least 2000 of them in the teaching of Jewish Rabbis before Christ). Jesus used parables to sift His hearers, some of whom just liked Jesus as a brilliant storyteller, and others who were on a spiritual search, and who could find God in the stories.

Dysfunctional families didn't die out after the New Testament period. There's a lot of family misery in the area where any of us live. As you read this, someone in your district is going through agony because of family problems. You could find a Battered Wives' Refuge within an easy distance of most of our towns or cities.. Estate agents in most areas are being pressurised to find far more two-bedroom flats than exist in most areas, because of the demand created by broken marriages. Any district is littered with broken promises, miserable couples and children or young people seething with resentment. The children find themselves in the most awful situations they never asked for. The strain on grandparents is killing them. A Scottish school-teacher was asked by a girl pupil whether he remembered her older sister who had left school the previous year. Then she told him her sister was expecting a baby . She and the lad who was the father of the child weren't married, but they had plans. 'It'll be alright, sir', she said reassuringly, ' My Mum is going to look after the baby till they get to know one another.' We are in a bit of a mess...

Suddenly this parable of Jesus, which Somerset Maughan the novelist called 'The greatest short story ever written', comes into focus. Here is the story. It occupies 22 verses in the New Testament , and takes three minutes to read aloud. This wonderful story, Luke's Gospel chapter 15, verses 11-31. Let's have it in fresh, up-dated language in Peterson's translation 'The Message' : 'Then Jesus said, 'There was once a man who had two sons. The younger said to his father, 'Father, I want right now what's coming to me.' So the father divided the property between them. It wasn't long before the younger son packed his bags and left for a distant country. There, undisciplined and dissipated, he wasted everything he had. After he had gone through all his money, there was a bad famine all through that country and he began to hurt. He signed on with a citizen there who assigned him to his fields to feed the pigs. He was so hungry he would have eaten the corn-cobs in the pig slop, but no one would give him any. That brought him to his senses. He said, 'All those farm-hands working for my father sit down to three meals a day, and here I am starving to death. I'm going back to my father. I'll say to him, 'Father, I've sinned against God , I've sinned before you; I don't deserve to be called your son. Take me on as a hired hand.' He got right up and went home to his father.

When he was still a long way off, his father saw him. His heart pounding, he ran out, embraced him, and kissed him. The son started his speech: 'Father, I've sinned against God, I've sinned before you; I don't deserve to be called your son ever again. '

But the father wasn't listening. He was calling to the servants, 'Quick. Bring a clean set of clothes and dress him. Put the family ring on his finger and sandals on his feet. Then get a grain-fed heifer and roast it. We're going to feast! We're going to have a wonderful time! My son is here – given up for dead and now alive! Given up for lost and now found! And they began to have a wonderful time.

All this time his older son was out in the field. When the day's work was done he came in. As he approached the house, he heard the music and the dancing. Calling over one of the houseboys, he asked what was going on. He told him, 'Your brother came home. Your father has ordered a feast – barbecued beef!- because he has him home safe and sound.'

The older brother stalked off in an angry sulk and refused to join in. His father came out and tried to talk to him, but he wouldn't listen. The son said, 'Look how many years I've stayed here serving you, never giving you one moment of grief, but have you ever thrown a party for me and my friends? Then this son of yours who has thrown away your money on prostitutes shows up, and you go all out with a feast!'

The father said, 'Son, you don't understand. You're with me all the time, and everything that is mine is yours – but this is a wonderful time, and we had to celebrate. This brother of yours was dead, and he's alive! He was lost, and he's found!'

It's a wonderful story, isn't it? An American negro preacher produced a neat analysis of it, with three main headings, each with three sub-headings. First of all, there was the Son's BADNESS – he revelled, he devilled and he grovelled. Secondly, there was the Son's SADNESS – he went to the dogs, he lost his togs, and he ate with the hogs. Thirdly, there was the Son's GLADNESS – he got the seal, he ate the veal, and he danced a reel... Enough of this badinage! We'll try to unpack natural detail from spiritual principle, and see how refreshingly up-to-date this story is.

Remember that the Bible has a mainly agricultural or pastoral background. At least twelve of Jesus' parables, like the Two Young Wasters, are related to farming. There's also a Jewish dimension to watch out for - imagine Jewish hearers cringing at the idea that the younger brother in the story was reduced to feeding pigs, which were an unclean animal to Jews. I remember once doing some Bible study (Genesis 22) with Glasgow children in my school classroom, and I asked a boy what Isaac offered up instead of his son, and I got the correct answer : 'A ram'. 'And what is a ram?' I asked politely. The boy replied, 'It's when two lorries crash into one another.' The kid was a city slicker and did not realise that a ram was a male animal with a head and horns at the front, a tail at the back, a leg at each corner and wool down the sides...Does it help to modernise the story? This lad was **SICK AT HOME**. In today's language, we would say the green wellies, Barbour jacket, Labrador dog and Volvo were not enough for him. He belonged to the 'I want it now' philosophy, amazingly similar to the plastic-based culture with which we are familiar. Things have changed; people used to save up for things, and buy into the principle of deferred gratification. They were willing to wait. Not so this lad. He grabbed everything he could, and tried to find fulfilment in material things.

When Bob Dylan visited John Lennon's house, he commented that Lennon had collected all sorts of bizarre objects, but would not be satisfied with them. If we are essentially spiritual beings, then we'll never satisfy spiritual need with material things. The lad in the story squandered his inheritance, and got no joy. His big brother was also **SICK AT HOME.** His heart was in turmoil – a seething mass of pent-up anger and smouldering resentment. He refused to recognise how near all the good things of home were to him, and was probably envious of his brother having what he imagined was a good time. Some people get so immersed in duty that they never have any joy. Do you know anyone like these two boys ? We'll try to find out how low this lad sank, his homesickness, and the way back...

Some people stress the unity of the whole chapter under the theme of lost-ness. We can be lost away from home, near home or at home. We can be lost through stupidity, carelessness, rebellion or duty. This parable has given hope to many people who have felt that they have strayed beyond the possibility of even God's recovery. If you feel like that this morning, be encouraged. There was once a young cooper from Wick called Jock Troup. He was so overcome by his sense of 'lost-ness', he told people later he was afraid to go to sleep at night in case he wakened up in hell...Through the help of the leaders at the Dublin YMCA he turned to God in the wheel-house of the boat he was serving in during the First World War, and found peace. Remember, talking isn't enough. Later in his life, when he was Superintendent of the Tent Hall in Glasgow, he showed God's kindness to the homeless men and women in Glasgow Green, as well as on the platform preaching to around eight hundred people, mainly men, every Sunday at the Free Breakfast for the Poor. During the Second World War, Jock Troup ran 'Services Suppers' for the young people passing through Glasgow on their way to take part in the horrors of war. Many of them must have felt lost.

In the blackness of his personal pigsty, the young waster made up speeches to deliver to his father when he got **HOME**. He had been sick at home, then home-sick, and now he was on the way home. The road to hell is paved with good intentions. The real hope starts when he stumbles to his feet and heads for his father and home. The sub-plots jump out of this story, and give the truth legs! Here is a wonderful image of repentance. The New Testament Greek word for repentance is 'metanoia' which means 'change-of-mind', but the Old Testament usage reminds us of the dynamics of repentance, for it is almost always a verb, a word of dynamic activity, a doing word in the Old Testament. Repentance is not simply being sorry for our sins. It is being sorry enough to give them up, to quit them. Repentance, in directional terms, is a U-turn. It means turning away from going our own way, to going towards God for His deliverance and help. A tourist in Ireland asked a local whether the road he was on would take him to Belfast. 'Sure, and it is', said the local, 'if you turn and go in the opposite direction!' When Jesus came preaching, the Gospels tell us He said: 'The kingdom of God is near. Repent and believe the Good News!' Repentance and faith go together. The Christian Good News is that when we take our first faltering steps towards God, we find Him running to meet us. The African scholar was right when he called this 'The Parable of the Waiting, Running and Embracing God.

There is a strange irony in the Parable of the Two Young Wasters. Everything which the younger brother left home to find was at home – satisfaction, supply, security and joy were all there, down on the farm, all the time! Over the years, preachers have pressed the details of the story to make this point. On his return, the Father smothers his younger son with love, and showers him with kindnesses. The joy of pardon is encapsulated in the details, which ring bells with other parts of the Bible. The **ROBE** is like the joy of salvation, for those who believe in Christ have put on Christ like a garment, as the apostle Paul writes in Colossians chapter three. In the same chapter, he reminds the believers that they have to discard the garments of their past, like filthy grave-clothes. One of the enduring symbols of the Book of Revelation is of the worshipping saints in heaven praising Jesus, wearing white robes. The **RING** is like the joy of sonship, pressed on wax to give a seal of authenticity. In John's Gospel chapter one, we read that 'as many as received Him, He gave the right (legitimate authority) to become children of God..' The **SHOES** speak of the joy of 'space', or freedom. 'Gimme space, man' has always been the young person's cry – room to breathe, room for manoeuvre, freedom from cramping circumstances. In the area of Machakos, Kenya, where I teach students every year, about one-quarter of the villagers have no footwear at all, and another quarter have only flip-flops. This is severely restrictive. Walking the two or three miles into Machakos on the dirt roads is a chore.
The cotton-pickin' negroes of the Southern States used to sing about shoes in their 'spirituals':

'I gotta shoes, you gotta shoes, all God's chillen gotta shoes,
    When I get to heaven, gonna put on my shoes, and walk all over God's
    heaven...'

The **CALF** in the story is like the joy of supper, which must have been tremendous for the starving young bundle of rags. This is all an image of satisfaction and supply, and God's provision of good things – daily bread and daily blessing – for those who love Him.

The final paragraph in the parable is a master-stroke, giving details of how the older brother felt.
The older brother had all of this 'on tap' as it were, but was still lost at home. I am sorry to tell you I have heard of, and met a few miserable people who go to church every Sunday, and who always seem to look as if God had died half an hour ago! Some of them enlist on the church door duty rota, and greet you with sepulchral tones, their clothing and appearance reminiscent of the

Addams Family! They seem to resent people they call 'strangers' or 'incomers' and 'outsiders', who find joy and peace from God among His church and His people.

Some of them were brought up in church and Sunday School, or even in Christian homes, but they are as bitter as the older brother in the parable. The intensity of his feelings come over in the terse and brilliantly-chosen words of the Lord Jesus: 'Look! All these years I've been slaving for you, and never disobeyed your orders. Yet you never gave me even a young goat so that I could celebrate with my friends.' None of his negative comments can undermine the Father's joy, which remains undiminished at the Prodigal's return. I write this as a waster who found God, and the discovery gave some insights into the Father's heart.

Some people think that the father in the story is too good to be true. The parable can be put into modern garb, and the father becomes a modern man who wins a large sum on the lottery, gives half to his son, who squanders the money in London (the most expensive city in the world, dearer than Hong Kong and New York) in a few months, and then reappears, penniless, at his parents' front door. If you told the parable like this to today's kids, and asked whether if they had done that, their father would welcome them back, how do you think they would respond? In a straw poll of about 250 thirteen year old children, a local teacher reported about half of them said they would be welcome, and the rest were a mixture of 'aye, you wish' -es, 'are you kiddings', and 'I'm not sures'!

There was a book written in the Buchan Doric of the North-East of Scotland called 'Sandy Scott's Bible Class' which features Sandy telling the parable of the two young wasters to his boys, and then asking them what they thought of that. 'Na, na,' said one boy, 'that's nae true tae nature, Sandy man.' 'Nae faither wid gie (would give) a daft response like that.'   Sandy said, 'It's nae true tae nature, son, but it is true tae grace. God is that kind o' faither.'

I am sure that Jesus meant to give us a lasting impression in this parable that Jesus meant us to understand that from this parable that this is what God is like. There are some who complain about this parable because it does not give the full picture of the Good News, especially because there is no symbolism of Jesus' crucifixion here. We could argue that no one parable can tell the full story, and we have to complement what is there with what is written elsewhere in the Bible.   It could also be argued that God was running to us in the Incarnation when Jesus was born, or in His compelling words and compassionate actions, including the Cross. I jotted down on the back of an envelope that it is easier to confess to God than to many a man, and that God is more merciful in His judgement than many men are. We were reading recently about a politician who won his court case and said he could never forgive his opponents at his trial. God can forgive where people refuse to forgive.
The best thing to do is to take steps toward Him, and see whether He comes running to meet us... He will!

QUESTIONS

1. Discuss what you think would be the best title for this parable?

2. Why is this parable so popular?

3. Why include the section about the elder brother? What would be the gain or loss by its omission?

4. The Prodigal Son was sick at home. Does he have any modern equivalents? Describe and discuss them?

5. The Prodigal Son was eventually homesick. How did he express this, and what proposed action did he take?

6. Is this parable true to nature? What percentage of parents today would welcome wayward young people who returned home seeking help? Does our society measure up to the father in this parable?

7. Is this parable theologically insufficient, because there is no equivalent to the Cross in it? Discuss.

CHAPTER 4

RICH AND FOOLISH.   Luke 12 v 13-21.

Someone in the crowd said to Jesus, 'Teacher, tell my brother to divide the inheritance with me.' Jesus replied, 'Man, who appointed me a judge or arbiter between you?' Then He said to them, 'Watch out! Be on your guard against all kinds of greed; a man's life does not consist in the abundance of his possessions.'
And He told them this parable: 'The ground of a certain rich man produced a good crop. He thought to himself, 'What shall I do? I have no place to store my crops.'
The he said, 'This is what I'll do. I will tear down my barns and build bigger ones, and there I will store all my grain and my goods. And I'll say to myself, 'You have plenty of good things laid up for many years. Take life easy; eat, drink and be merry.'
But God said to him, 'You fool! This night your life will be demanded from you. Then who will get what you have prepared for yourself?'

'This is how it will be for anyone who stores up things for himself but is not rich towards God.'

RICH AND FOOLISH.

This parable is another story, not of country folk, but of a country person who was a bit like somebody called Edith, of whom it was said 'Edith lived in a little world bordered on the North, South East and West by Edith.' The keynote warning is against greed of all kinds (verse 15).

This country person was a farmer who featured in one of Jesus' parables, and unlike the parable of the Two Young Wasters, there is no mention of wife, children or servants, or anyone else. He lives by himself, and he talks to himself, and thinks and plans only in relation to himself. It seems so unnatural. We are naturally mixers, not loners. Someone pointed out that Tarzan of the Apes is an impossible fiction – we are by nature gregarious creatures, and everything we do has repercussions. JS Whale said that there are cosmic repercussions when a child throws a teddy bear out of his pram! We need to respond to our fellow-humans; it's like the pebbles on the beach rattling into one another, and becoming smooth and rounded.

Try telling all this to the man in today's parable, and he would chase you off his farm!

In the immediate context of Luke's Gospel chapter 12 in which this parable occurs, Jesus asks a question, issues a warning, and states a principle. When someone in the crowd asked Jesus to tell his brother to divide the family inheritance with him, Jesus asked : 'Who appointed me a judge or arbiter between you?' Then Jesus issued a general warning against all kinds of greed, and finally stated a principle that 'life is not defined by what you have, even when you have a lot'.

To drive home His teaching, Jesus told the Parable of the Greedy Farmer, or The Rich Fool, a totally self-centred individual, who got a rude awakening... The parable has six verses and can be read in just about one minute flat. Here it is in Petersen's translation, 'The Message'.

'Then Jesus told them this story: 'The farm of a certain rich man produced a terrific crop. He talked to himself: 'What can I do? My barn isn't big enough for this harvest! Then he said, 'Here's what I'll do. I'll tear down my barns and build bigger ones. Then I'll gather in all my grain and goods, and I'll say to myself, 'Self, you've done well! You've got it made and can now retire. Take it easy and have the time of your life! 'Just then God showed up and said, 'Fool! Tonight you die. And your barnful of goods – who gets it?' 'That's what happens when you fill your barn with Self and not with God.'

At least ten of Jesus' parables centre around money, and no wonder. One scholar has said that the Jews in Israel at the time of Jesus were the heaviest taxed nation ever in the history of the world. People were paying to feed their families. They were also paying for the upkeep of the local synagogue, and Herod's ambitious building project, the Jerusalem Temple. They were paying a ferry tax to cross the Sea of Galilee. They also paid taxes for the upkeep of the hated occupying force, the Roman Army. The licences to collect provincial taxes were auctioned to the 'tax farmers' in Rome annually, and right down the line the publicani, or tax collectors were piling on extras.

That is why Jewish tax-collectors like Zaccheus, whom we read about in Luke chapter 19 were regarded as quislings and traitors. This also explains why it was the most stinging insult to say that Jesus was the 'friend of tax-collectors (publicans) and sinners'. One of the taxes most hated by the Jews was the frontier tax, which had to be paid by travellers when crossing national boundaries, and which fluctuated enormously. Imagine going your holidays, and not knowing whether you had enough money to reach the country you were going to! Money for accommodation and spending was additional to that. That's how a Jew felt travelling to Jerusalem for the Passover Festival....The Jews were paying about eleven, some think thirteen, different taxes.

Therefore, when Jesus spoke about money, everybody listened. Thinking about money is a universal pastime. Ray Charles said that affluence separates people, but poverty knits them together. Joe Louis said everything costs a lot of money when you haven't got any. Martin Luther King Junior said in a speech in 1958 'In all your material wealth, you are spiritually and morally poverty-stricken, unable to speak to the conscience of the world.'
Jesus addresses a church in the Book of Revelation: ' You say I am rich; I have acquired wealth and do not need a thing.' But you do not realize that you are wretched, poor, pitiful, blind and naked. I counsel you to buy from me gold refined in the fire so that you can become rich; and white clothes to wear, so that you can cover your shameful nakedness; and salve to put on your eyes, so you can see.'
The rich person thinks about his next million, the poor person thinks about his next meal. I speak as someone who was a poor child in Glasgow, a frequenter of pawnshops, rag-stores and scrap metal merchants. We'll have a dig into what motivated this wealthy farmer.

The parables of Jesus, as we saw earlier, were a teaching tool to sift the hearers into those who had a merely superficial interest in someone they might regard as a community story-teller, and those who were on a spiritual search for God, and were keen to look under the surface of the story for spiritual reality. The first thing we notice when we look at this parable is this farmer's
SLAVERY IN RELATION TO THE PAST He was thirled to things, and motivated by money. (the old Scots verb 'to thirl' means 'to hold in bondage, or servitude'). William Barclay quoted the Romans, who said money was like sea-water; the more you drink, the thirstier you became. Have you met folk like that? One of my work-mates used to borrow my Christmas edition of the Radio and TV Times so that he could copy them on the office photocopier and save money over Christmas! Another of my well-heeled acquaintances used to take money from his mother for driving her a few miles into the railway station. Some folk get so involved in the paper money chase, that if you asked them how much was enough they would probably say 'always a little more.' It is sometimes said that the Bible says 'money is the root of all evil.' That is NOT correct. The Bible says 'the LOVE of money is the root of all evil.'
Some 'professionals' won't move a muscle unless they get a fee for it. I was once asked to conduct a funeral service for a dog. I refused, not because of financial reasons, because the lady said she would pay me handsomely. I gave her a name and a phone number, and commented to my son 'he would murder his granny for ten pounds, never mind take a dog's funeral.'
Greed and selfishness go together. A friend of mine shared his economic theory one day. He said we should get all the money in the world and put it all

in a great pile. Then we should divide it out so that everyone got an equal amount. Then he said that when his pile was spent, we should do the same all over again!

The farmer here suffered from I disease, spelt capital I. In the story we have 5 'I's, 2 'Selfs', and 4 'my's. He seemed to have too much ego in his cosmos. He obviously could not harvest the bumper crop on his own, yet he speaks of it all as if it were all due to his efforts. What about the workers?! They would probably echo the sentiments expressed by an Upper Clyde Shipbuilders' shop steward some years ago: 'The bosses in this company are preventing the work force from fulfilling their full potential.'

Money can be a good servant, but it is a bad master. It can also be an obstacle in our service and worship of God. Jesus said that no-one can serve two masters, for either he will love the one, and hate the other, or else be loyal to one and despise the other. Jesus said we cannot serve both God and money (or anything else). The Book of Deuteronomy says it is the Lord who gives us power to earn money. We have to exercise a sacred stewardship of everything we have. The farmer in this parable didn't see it like that.

We have looked at the farmer with respect to his slavery in relation to the past. Now we'll look at his:

STUPIDITY IN RELATION TO THE FUTURE. Now, he wasn't all bad. Consider some of his good points. He seemed to be honest and diligent. Jesus doesn't say anywhere that he got his bumper crop dishonestly or illegally. Secondly, he has to be praised for his industry and effort. He worked hard and long to achieve this target. There's no doubt that he was a good manager, using the best of seed, probably good quality workers and the most up-to-date methods. He was not a workaholic, killing himself and others around him on the job. He was a planner, preparing for a happy retirement. However, he made some very serious errors. In His teaching on the Sermon on the Mount, Jesus warns against calling people fools. Yet in this story, God calls this man a fool. What makes a man (or woman) a fool? Well, there are at least three components :

Firstly, They mistake themselves for God. They refuse to acknowledge the existence of God, and run their lives as if He did not exist. It's actually more serious than that. Someone was described as a self-made man who worshipped his own creator.

Secondly, they mistake their body for their soul. How prone we are to pamper our bodies. The advertisers wouldn't spend all that money promoting soap, shower gel, anti-ageing creams, hair dye, and a million other beauty aids if there weren't customers so concerned about appearance and image. Yet how much do we spend to develop the spiritual dimension of life, to consider the factors in our planet's existence which would indicate a friendly Creator, or to evaluate how we could discover and respond to Him? The Bible's teaching is not so much that each one of us has a soul as that each one of us IS a soul? What do you think of Jesus? Was He bad, sad, mad, or God? We are essentially spiritual beings, made with a Godward reference. That is why worship is such a world-wide phenomenon.

Thirdly, they mistake time for eternity. Their theme song is: 'I'm gonna live for ever.' We are experts at dodging the idea of ageing. I knew a lady who

deliberately cleared all the mirrors out of her house. The farmer in Jesus' story had no plans for handover...In the Cowcaddens district of Glasgow, there used to be a carving on top of a building : 'Tak' Tent o' Time ere Time be Tent,' which being translated means 'Pay attention to Time before Time is Over'. In his letter to the Corinthian church, the Apostle Paul says that the things which are seen are temporary, but the things that are unseen are eternal. There is an old Christian rhyme which says:
Only one life, 'twill soon be past,
Only what's done for Jesus will last.

Muhammad Ali (some of you may remember him as Cassius Clay) said that all the wealth on this earth, all the wealth under the earth, and all the wealth in the universe is like a mosquito's wing compared to the wealth we will receive in the hereafter.

Two Jewish rabbis were discussing when would be the best time to repent. 'I know when,' one of them said. 'The best time would be the day before you die.' 'There's only one problem with that,' said the other rabbi. 'You don't know when you're going to die, so you don't know when is the best time to repent.' 'Well,' said the first rabbi, 'Now we've solved the problem, because if you don't know when you're going to die, the best time to repent is today.'

The American evangelist Billy Graham is one of the world's top 100 best-known people. He was visiting a rich farmer (you've noticed the connection with our parable?) who was trying to impress him that he was a man of power and wealth. 'You see all the land in this direction, Billy? I own it.' 'And you see all the land up to that fence a mile away? That's my land. And you see all the land stretching as far as the homestead on that faraway hill? I've owned it for forty years. And the land stretching over to the horizon is my territory too.' Billy Graham pointed vertically to the sky. 'How much do you own in this direction, my friend? The Bible says we have to lay up treasure in heaven, because where our treasure is, there will our heart be also...'
The rich fool in Jesus' story was not interested in searching for God's kingdom and glory, either in this life or the life to come, and that was very sad. In Matthew chapter 6 and verse 33 it says we should steep our lives in God-reality, God-initiative, and God-provisions, and not worry about missing out. It says then we'll find all our everyday human concerns will be met. Note thirdly:

THE PARABLE'S SOLEMNITY IN RELATION TO THE PRESENT.

We've looked at the farmer's slavery to things and money in relation to his past, and his stupidity in relation to the future, despite his good points. In the final analysis, the parable conveys a strong solemnity in relation to his present.
At first glance, there seems to be a strong contrast between the prosperous farmer in Jesus' parable, and today's world.
The most powerful drug in our society isn't alcohol or heroin, it's hedonism, or pleasure-seeking. Watch any police documentary on weekend activity and under-age drinking in any city centre in Britain, and you'll see groups of kids dressed up and raring to go and spend, spend, spend, like there was no

tomorrow. A whole genre of TV documentaries has been spawned showing experts involved in the plight of people in deep debt because they refuse to be disciplined about their spending. It isn't only youngsters, and it isn't only spenders who are responsible. High Street traders, banks, building societies and credit-card companies are turning us into a nation of debt-junkies. Worrying about debt has turned us into a nation of insomniacs – that's why the TV programmes go on through the night.

A group of consumer studies students were let loose in Princes Street, Edinburgh, were instructed to tell the truth about their financial state, and encouraged to see how much credit they would be offered. The results were staggering. Each one could have had thousands of pounds – to 'live now'. Arguably the three most powerful lessons in the parable are **the brevity of life, the reality of God**, and **the urgency of repentance**. Time comes to us whizzing out of the future, has a brief brush with the present, and is past before we know it. I have moved from life with paraffin lamps, coal fires, outside dry lavatories and linoleum, to life with central heating, e-mails and text messages, and international air travel. In August I wanted to know who hijacked July! Yet the farmer and my contemporaries are living as if life and lifetimes were endless. Each one of us should be thinking: 'I have only one life, and God has only one me.' A minister friend of mine was questioning a family recently about their mother so that he could say something about her at her funeral. The one thing they kept repeating was 'Oh, she liked caramel sweets'. He went away feeling sad that this was all they could say about the dear lady.

One day this selfish greedy farmer had to face God, and hear God's verdict on his life. That is a very solemn thing we should all think about, and take remedial action. The urgency for the need for repentance, and faith, should be pressing in on us, so that we enter into the kind of life Jesus intends for us. In Luke chapter 13 verse 15, Jesus is reported as using the Greek word 'zoe' for 'life'. He could have used 'bios', which is merely animal existence, but 'zoe' is essential and full life, life with a capital L. Jesus said 'I have come that they might have life, and life to the full.'

QUESTIONS

1. What is Jesus warning us against in this parable? Give a one-word answer!

2. Discuss the commendable points about the farmer in the parable?

3. What serious omissions were there in his attitudes, work and planning?

4. See Matthew 5 verses 21 – 22. Is it good to call someone a fool? Why does God call this man a fool?

5. Discuss the role and limitations of hard work, saving and forward planning in our lives.

CHAPTER 5

2 PRAYER PARABLES.   LUKE 18 V 1-14.

Then Jesus told His disciples a parable to show them that they should always pray and not give up. He said: 'In a certain town there was a judge who neither feared God nor cared about men. And there was a widow in that town who kept coming to him with the plea, 'Grant me justice against my adversary.'

For some time he refused. But finally he said to himself, 'Even though I don't fear God or care about men, yet because this widow keeps bothering me, I will see that she gets justice, so that she won't eventually wear me out with her coming!'

And the Lord said, 'Listen to what the unjust judge says. And will not God bring about justice for His chosen ones, who cry out to him day and night? Will He keep putting them off? I tell you, He will see that they get justice, and quickly. However, when the Son of Man comes, will He find faith on the earth?'

To some who were confident of their own righteousness and looked down on everybody else, Jesus told this parable: 'Two men went up to the Temple to pray, one a Pharisee and the other a tax collector. The Pharisee stood up and prayed about himself : 'God, I thank You that I am not like other men – robbers, evildoers, adulterers – or even like this tax collector. I fast twice a week and give a tenth of all I get.' But the tax collector stood at a distance. He would not even look up to heaven, but beat his breast and said, 'God, have mercy on me, a sinner.'

'I tell you that this man, rather than the other, went home justified before God. For everyone who exalts himself will be humbled, and he who humbles himself will be exalted.'

TWO PRAYER PARABLES.

Parables are teaching stories about ordinary life, with spiritual overtones. In this chapter, we're looking at two parables about prayer.

Andrew Macbeath, a former Principal of the Bible Training Institute in Bothwell Street, Glasgow, was once a theological student at New College, Edinburgh. He went to take his first exams, and the papers were given out, when a student put up his hand. 'Yes, what is it?' the invigilator asked. The student asked why they had prayer before every lecture, but no prayer before exams. The invigilator responded in clipped tones, 'No outside help is permitted in examinations.' The Christian view on prayer is that we all need Outside Help, from God, in the examinations of life, and the strongest arguments for prayer are first of all, that Jesus prayed, and secondly that Jesus gave clear teaching about prayer.

In Luke's Gospel, Jesus had given earlier teaching on prayer in chapter 11. In response to a request to teach His disciples to pray, He gave them a template for prayer in what we normally call the Lord's Prayer, followed by the Parable of the Friend at Midnight, and an illustration of the Father and Son.... We are going to look at Jesus' deft word-pictures in Luke chapter 18. The first one is the **Parable of the Persistent Widow,** and the second one is the **Parable of the Pharisee and the Publican.** Or my preferred title, the **Parable of the Poser and the Penitent.** Here comes the first of these from Luke 18 verses 1-8, in Peterson's translation. 'The Message.':
Jesus told them a story showing that it was necessary for them to pray consistently and never quit. He said, 'There was once a judge in some city who never gave God a thought and cared nothing for people. A widow in that city kept after him: 'My rights are being violated. Protect me!'
He never gave her the time of day.

But after this went on and on he said to himself, 'I care nothing what God thinks, even less what people think. But because this widow won't quit badgering me, I'd better do something and see that she gets justice – otherwise I'm going to end up beaten black and blue by her pounding.'

Then the Master said, 'Do you hear what that judge, corrupt as he is, is saying? So what makes you think God won't step in and work justice for His chosen people, who continue to cry out for help? Won't He stick up for them? I assure you, He will. He will not drag His feet. But how much of that kind of persistent faith will the Son of Man find on the earth when He returns?'

When we look at life through the parables, or teaching stories of Jesus, we discover that these two parables are the only ones in the Gospels which state the reason why they were given before the parable is set out. The target here is consistency and persistence in prayer. If the teaching in Luke chapter 18 was given at the same time as the narrative in chapter 17, then Jesus is looking for consistency in the light of His future coming and judgement.

The first parable here is about a judge. The legal profession has always had a bad press, and it is the same here. I heard about someone who read a tombstone which said 'Here lies a solicitor, and an honest man', and said 'Oh, are there two people buried in there?' There was a competition recently in the North of England to find the biggest liar on earth, and politicians and lawyers were not allowed to enter.

Justice was hard to come by in the times of Herod the Great, a vicious tyrant who killed off large numbers of his own family. The Emperor Augustine said it was safer to be Herod's pig than his son. The judge in Jesus' story 'never gave God a thought, and cared nothing for people.' He was neither religious nor humanitarian, and didn't give a fig for this feisty widow who kept shouting for justice, and tormenting the judge. He eventually bent like a tree in a hurricane before her onslaught, ignored his normal responses, and procured justice for her, so that he could procure peace for himself. Like so many in today's world, the widow felt exploited, oppressed and humiliated. She feels like the Canaanite woman whose visit to Jesus is recorded in Matthew chapter 15, who regards herself as a 'dog' until Jesus intervenes and shows her that she is a daughter. Sometimes we are called to go through dark hours, which destroy our self-confidence. Persistent prayer makes us like George Matheson the hymn writer:
'I see the rainbow through the rain, and feel the promise is not vain that morn shall tearless be.'

When we 'pray through', we find a kindness in God and His Word which is the sweet and nourishing core of the Good News.
God is the special champion of the weak and the underprivileged, the refugees, widows and orphans, and all those without clout. The Old Testament prophets had justice as a major theme. John McFadyen's commentary on the Book of the prophet Amos is entitled 'A Cry for Justice.' The most superficial look at the AIDs epidemic in Africa, the ruthless exploitation of cheap labour and child labour, the hangovers from the caste system in India, and the ruinous effect of tribalism on talent should make us cry for God's intervention.

Some folk think that Jesus is giving teaching by contrast here. They argue that we have here what is called a 'how much more' argument. The drift of it is this: if an unjust judge can be badgered into intervening by the constant moaning of a pesky widow, how much more will a loving Heavenly Father intervene on behalf of His children who call on Him?
We have to keep on praying and seeking and asking for God's intervention, especially on behalf of others. An old Scots golf manual had as its final instruction: 'Finally, never give up: your opponent might die!'
An African commentator writes: 'The fact that God became incarnate in Jesus Christ gives us confidence that he sides with the afflicted, the oppressed and the desperate and plans to exalt them.'

Luke's Gospel reveals a special interest in the prayer life of Jesus. He seems to be steeped in prayer. Luke records nine prayers of Jesus, of which all but two are found in no other Gospel. These prayers are associated with important events – at His baptism, after a day of miracles, before choosing His disciples, before His first prediction of His Passion, at the Transfiguration, on the return of the seventy from evangelistic mission, before teaching the disciples how to pray, in the Garden of Gethsemane, and on the Cross. Once,

Luke tells us, He withdrew into a desert (chapter 5 verse 16), and once He spends a whole night in prayer (chapter 6 v 12). Three of Luke's special parables deal with prayer – the friend at midnight, the persistent widow and the poser and the penitent. Luke alone includes Jesus' special prayer for Peter – 'Simon, Simon, Satan has desired to have you (all), but I have prayed for you (particularly) , and when you are converted, strengthen your brothers.' (Luke 22v31,32). Luke alone tells us that Jesus exhorted the disciples to pray in Gethsemane. He prayed for His enemies, and for Himself (22v41).

He sought out and loved to be in quiet places (4v42, a lonely place), quiet towns (9v10 – to Bethsaida) and hillsides – He went out to spend the night on the hill called the Mount of Olives (Luke 31v37).

I wrote at the start that the strongest argument for prayer on our part is that Jesus prayed. If Jesus was the Son of God, who enjoyed an unbroken fellowship with His Father God, except for a brief period on the Cross, then surely that presents a strong case that we should pray.

Prayer changes things, and people, including those who pray. Try an experiment. Think of someone you really don't like, and try praying for them every day. Review the situation on a weekly basis, and note any changes in attitude or behaviour on their part and yours...

Someone has produced a helpful acrostic on the components of prayer, based on the word 'acts' - Adoration, Confession, Thanksgiving, and Supplication. The negro spirituals sometimes contain helpful doggerel **and** good theology: 'You can talk about me as much as you please,
I'll talk about you down upon my knees!'

We are looking at Jesus' teaching on prayer from two parables in Luke's Gospel, chapter 18. The second parable is known widely as the Parable of the Pharisee and the Publican. I would prefer to call it The Parable of the Poser and the Penitent. Here is Peterson's translation of Jesus' words in 'The Message' :

He told His next story to some who were complacently pleased with themselves over their moral performance and looked down their noses at the common people: 'Two men went up to the Temple to pray, one a Pharisee and the other a tax man. The Pharisee posed and prayed like this: 'Oh, God, I thank You that I am not like other people – robbers , crooks, adulterers, or, heaven forbid, like this tax man. I fast twice a week and tithe all my income.' Meanwhile the tax man, slumped in the shadows, his face in his hands, not daring to look up, said, 'God, give mercy. Forgive me, a sinner.' Jesus commented, 'This tax man, not the other went home made right with God. If you walk around with your nose in the air, you're going to end up flat on your face, but if you're content to be simply yourself, you will become more than yourself.'

The scholars argue about the meaning of the word 'Pharisee', but the majority opinion is it means 'Separatist'. The Pharisees would trace their spiritual pedigree back to the Hasidim or Loyalists, who stood apart during the Maccabbean revolt in the second century BC, and fought against the Seleucid King Antiochus Epiphanes, who captured Jerusalem, and offered pig-meat on the Jerusalem altar. By the time of Jesus, there were about six thousand of them. They were orthodox, devout Jews. Today we would call them a fundamentalist Bible study group-cum-lunch-club with a down on women. I'd better not link them to any modern Christian group or I could be involved in a law-suit! They loved and studied the Old Testament, and especially the first five books of the Law, the Torah or Pentateuch (Genesis to Deuteronomy in the Bible). They also studied the teaching of generations of Jewish scholars. They believed that God spent several hours a day studying the Torah, just to keep up to date...

They were an elitist group who despised the 'people of the land', but regarded it as a God-given task to try and convert the whole nation into a good spiritual state. If the nation could only keep the Law of God for one day, then they said God would send the Deliverer, or Messiah.

Let's look at one of them in action in the Temple.

Jesus' story of the Poser and the Penitent is very penetrating and challenging. Jesus told this story to those who were 'complacently pleased with themselves', and He sets it in the Temple, noting the contrast of two men at prayer. This parable, like several of Luke's parables, has proved to be a great favourite through the years, and our national bard Robert Burns, was so taken with it that he wrote 'Holy Willie's Prayer' as a kind of flattering Presbyterian parallel:

'I bless and praise Thy matchless might, when thousands Thou hast left in night, that I am here, afore Thy sight for gifts an' grace, a burning and a shining light to a' this place...'

'Yet I am here, a chosen sample, to show Thy grace is great and ample,
I'm here a pillar in Thy Temple, strong as a rock,
A guide a buckler , and example to a' Thy flock...'

For some people, religion is a kind of whitewash, rather than a heart relationship with Jesus as Saviour. Jesus called the Pharisees 'whitewashed tombs, full of dead men's bones'. The heart of the Gospel is inner relationship, not outward religion. People like the man in the story are posers. Jesus had personal attitude in mind here. This man was smug as he thought of his outward conformity to Old Testament Law, summarised in the Ten Commandments. This promoted a snooty attitude towards those who were too busy trying to make ends meet, and who didn't have time to engage in all their outward observance. The Pharisees would classify them as 'the rest', or 'the people of the land', and write them of as despised also-rans. The two men here both went to the Temple, and they both went to pray. There the similarity ends. The Poser's prayer was delivered by a man standing proudly, purring with self-satisfaction, and his prayer never clears the ceiling. As he points the finger of accusation at others for their sins, there are three pointing at himself. A few of his tribe are still alive:

'I once met a Christian, a peacock so proud,
His vanity showed through the holes in his shroud.'

His claims about his fasting and tithing went far beyond the call of duty, and the Torah, and if we accept the teaching of Jesus at face value, the value of his sacrifices was wiped out by his making a public show of them.

Jesus struck a keynote of secrecy, so that only God knew about such devotion. Tithing is the giving of one-tenth of our income to religious causes. Nowadays, thanks to the generosity of our Government, Christian giving can be enhanced by 28 pence in the pound through Gift Aid...In the light of this, we'd better have a look at the tax man.

I constantly wonder at the story-telling skill of Jesus. He obviously included the tax man here in this parable, not simply to point out what sincerity in prayer and true penitence were like, but also to highlight the disgusting character of prudish religion, epitomised in Jesus' description of the Pharisee. Jesus is also underlining the objective of the story set out before it was told, 'to some who were complacently pleased with themselves.' The Pharisee probably flaunted himself as near the altar as he could be, as Jesus said elsewhere, 'to be seen by others'. In a previous broadcast I mentioned that the Jews in the time of Jesus were possibly the most taxed nation ever, paying at least eleven, possibly thirteen different kinds of taxes.

Tax collectors, or 'publicani' (Translated misleadingly for our culture as 'publicans' in the King James Version of the Bible) were regarded as the scum of the earth, quislings, self-seekers, collaborators and traitors. Zaccheus in Luke chapter 19 was one. The tax man in this story knew his position, and slunk in to a back corner seat in the Temple. His whole attitude reveals the demeanour of a penitent. The Pharisee's prayer was full of capital I's. The grammar changes with the tax man, who goes into object case, 'God be merciful to **me**, a sinner'. The tax man slumps in the shadows, his body language indicating self-humiliation, 'face in his hands, not daring to look up.'

There is a rich vocabulary of sin in the range of words used in the Old Testament. Sin is Deficiency or coming short of God's glory...Sin is Deviation, a basic crookedness in human nature...Sin is Disobedience to God's holy character and laws...Sin is Defilement, an impure affront against God's holiness.... Sin is Defiance, a mutinous rebellion against the Lordship of Jesus....At its root, all sin is fundamentally against God. When King David's sin is exposed to him through the parable of the Pet Lamb told by Nathan the prophet, David doesn't say 'I have sinned against Bathsheba by committing adultery with her' or 'I have sinned against Uriah, Bathsheba's husband, by planning that he should be killed in the battle'. David says 'I have sinned **against the LORD.**'

The Penitent tax man in this parable has two very strong convictions. The first one is that God is compassionate and merciful, so he says, 'God, grant mercy'. The verb here repeats God's act of mercy on the Day of Atonement, when the nation's sins were forgiven as the high priest sprinkled blood on the 'mercy seat', and confessed their sins over the scapegoat, then hunted it into the desert. This 'mercy seat' was the lid of the Ark of the Covenant, which became the focus of God's mercy. In Romans 3 v 25, Paul says 'God presented Him (Christ Jesus) as a sacrifice of atonement through faith in His blood.'

The Penitent's second conviction is that he is a sinner. The Greek text actually says 'to me **the** sinner', as if he is specifying himself as singled out from other sinners, as the sinner par excellence, hence the definite article.

There is a pitfall to avoid, and an example to follow in this parable. An American preacher from Boston fell at the pitfall, when he preached about ths parable, and then prayed: 'Lord, we thank You that we are not like this Pharisee', which was simply perpetuating the error. The example to follow is an up-dated attitude of the Penitent Tax Collector, where we should bow before the Cross of Jesus, and plead for God's mercy. Humility is a duty, not a grace. It is a right response to our sinful condition before God, rather than a gift God gives us.

QUESTIONS

1. 'Prayer is a presumptuous waste of time – Que sera, sera, and there's nothing you can do about it.' Discuss.

2. Is the parable about the widow an encouragement to bombard God with repeated prayer requests, or is it a 'how much more parable'? ie if an unfair judge eventually responded to a pestilential lady, how much more will He answer your prayers. Discuss.

3. Can you give any examples of people who prayed persistently about circumstances or people and received positive answers?

4. Are there any rules for praying? Discuss whether there are, and what They are.

5. Does God only answer the prayers of 'His chosen ones' (Luke 18 verse 7), or does He answer the prayers of unbelievers? Discuss.

6. What is God's attitude to pride? Is humility something God gives us as a gift, or is it a proper response to who God is? In other words, is humility a grace or a duty (See Galatians 5 verse 22-23 where humility is missing, and 1 Peter 5 verse 5-7)

7. Is our attitude reflected in our posture at prayer? Is it better to kneel?

8. What have you found helpful in praying that you could pass on?

9. How do you understand the phrase 'justified before God' (Luke 18 verse 14)

CHAPTER 6

RICH MAN, POOR MAN   Luke 16 v19-31

There was a rich man who was dressed in fine linen and lived in luxury every day. At his gate was laid a beggar named Lazarus, covered with sores and longing to eat what fell from the rich man's table. Even the dogs came and licked his sores.

The time came when the beggar died and the angels carried him to Abraham's side. The rich man also died and was buried. In hell, where he was in torment, he looked up and saw Abraham far away, with Lazarus by his side. So he called to him. 'Father Abraham, have pity on me and send Lazarus to dip the tip of his finger in water and cool my tongue, for I am in agony in this fire.'

But Abraham replied, 'Son, remember that in your lifetime you received your good things, while Lazarus received bad things, but now he is comforted here and you are in agony. And besides all this, between us and you a great chasm has been fixed, so that those who want to go from here to you cannot, nor can anyone cross over from there to us.'

He answered, 'Then I beg you, father, send Lazarus to my father's house, for I have five brothers. Let him warn them, so that they will not come also to this place of torment.'

Abraham replied, 'They have Moses and the Prophets; let them listen to them.'

'No, Father Abraham,' he said, 'but if someone from the dead goes to them, they will repent.'

He said to him, 'If they do not listen to Moses and the Prophets, they will not be convinced even if someone rises from the dead.'

RICH MAN, POOR MAN

I have conducted a good number of funerals and cremations in my ministry, and I know there is a great interest in what some people call 'the other side', or 'life after death'. Today's parable is not well known, and has been called 'The Parable of the Rich Man and Lazarus', or the 'Parable of Dives (Latin for 'rich') and Lazarus.' William Barclay calls it 'the Parable of the Man who Never Noticed.'

Some folk have wondered whether it is a parable, since it is not named as such, and it would be the only parable which contains a proper name. Not all parables are named as such, and the proper name here has a special reason for being there, so to me it's an OK parable. Willie Barclay says it is constructed with such masterly skill that not one phrase is wasted.

The Old Testament book of Job asks 'If a man dies, shall he live again?', and lots of folk say 'no' and heave a sigh of relief. Most folk fear death as the King of Terrors and the Terror of Kings, the Grim Reaper, or according to John Milton, 'The blind fate with the abhorred shears who cuts the thin-spun life'. Martin Luther King Junior said: 'The only way we can really achieve freedom is to somehow conquer the fear of death. For if a man has not discovered something he can die for, he is not fit to live.' Desmond Tutu said 'What can you do about death? You have to go on. I work on the basis that I'm doing God's work, and it's His business to look after me. Nobody is indispensable.' Bernard Shaw said that if we were going to die, we should die doing what we love to do. Job said 'I know that my Redeemer lives, and that He will stand at the latter day upon the earth. And though worms destroy this body, yet in my flesh shall I see God.'

People tell us that no one has ever come back to tell us what death is like, yet nowadays there are people who claim point-of-death experiences.
When people are killed by the roadside, in recent years it has been the custom to lay out bunches of flowers beside where they were killed. Some people say that good dead people turn into angels. Did Jesus have anything to say about all this? Yes, He did! Although it is a bit scary to read about hell, torment, agony and fire, today's parable sets out some important principles in relation to **two men in their lives, their deaths and their differences.** The parable is not the whole story, but it says enough for us to be clear, and know what remedial action, if any, has to be taken....

1. TWO MEN IN THEIR LIVES.

There is the greatest possible contrast between the lifestyle of the rich man and the lifestyle of Lazarus the beggar.

It is very difficult for us to imagine what it was like to be poor in the time of Jesus. There was no welfare or Social Security, unlike today, when as one wag said Jehovah Jireh (the Lord will provide) has been replaced by Jehovah Giro. Also, our view of poverty varies enormously within our own culture. The students at Eton were once asked to write an essay on

Poverty, and one of them wrote: 'Once upon a time, there was a poor family. The Mummy was poor, the Daddy was poor. All the children were poor – even the butler was poor...'

Time affects people's view of poverty. The plight of the poor in Britain has changed since the nineteenth century, as when the shocking conditions at the Andover Workhouse were exposed in 1845. In this idyllic part of Hampshire, the drunken supervisor frequently fought with his horrible wife. He thrashed children as young as three for messing their beds, and some of the paupers in the place kept alive by eating candles. One wretched resident remembered his children eating the potato peelings thrown out for the supervisor's chickens.

Now consider Lazarus in our story. He was laid at the rich man's gate, presumably by some helper, for as Ray Charles said, poverty knits people together. He was probably too weak to walk there. Unlike the rich man, Jesus does not describe his clothing. His only covering was the collection of suppurating sores, a mantle of weeping wounds which covered his emaciated body. There is no definite word that he actually got any food. He was hopeful for the fallout and the handout from the rich man's table, as his guests would wipe their hands on pieces of bread, and then throw them away.
Lazarus was too weak to ward off the dogs in the street.
When we read about dogs here, we must remember that there were two kinds of dogs: pet dogs and pariah dogs. The parable is not describing the pampered lap-dogs of the rich, but the mangy scroungers of the backstreets, which you will find in any big city today. In Sao Paolo, Brazil, I used to go for the milk and rolls each morning armed with a short aluminium clothes-pole to fend them off. I have heard of church workers in Glasgow housing estates being trapped and then rescued by small boys on stair landings. One man told about looking through a letter-box, and seeing the matted hair, the wild red eyes, the yellow teeth and the slobbering mouth, and he said that was just the woman – you should have seen the dog!

Back to our parable... These unclean animals licked Lazarus' sores, and his abject state meant that he was helpless to fight them off. Another way of looking at it was that this was a touch of brute pity in the absence of any human help.

Let us now consider:

2. **TWO MEN IN THEIR DEATHS**.

Lazarus gets first mention. He was probably given the most cursory treatment and the simplest of 'send-offs', (I know an African who recently buried his father, total cost £50), but in the words of Jesus, 'the beggar died, and the angels carried him to Abraham's side.'
As a diseased and destitute beggar, the body of Lazarus would probably be dumped in the Valley of Hinnom, the constantly burning refuse heap in Jerusalem. It had been kept like that ever since its desecration by good

King Josiah, in the seventh century BC. Prior to that, it was a shrine dedicated to the pagan god Molech, where child sacrifice took place – see 2 Kings 23 verse 10.

The imagery of being at Abraham's side is of a meal at a low table, with people reclining on their left elbows on a couch, so that one person's head came near the chest or side of the other. Abraham was the Father of the Jewish nation, so to be at his side was to be in the paradise of God.
No doubt the pomp and pride which accompanied the rich man in life would accompany him to his grandiose tomb. I was reminded of the doggerel:
'Here lies James Bracket, in his fancy wooden jacket,
He lived like a hog, and died like a dog,
And left all his riches to fools...'

Try to imagine the speeches at the rich man's funeral. Sometimes at funerals, you scarcely recognise the goods from the description. There is the greatest possible contrast between not only the destination, but the state of the two men. Lazarus is relaxing beside Abraham, and the Rich man is suffering the torments of Hades, characterised by discomfort, thirst, and fire. There isn't a fully-developed doctrine of the after-life in the Old Testament. Hades (the word in the Greek text of our parable) was a kind of shadow-land where people live in limbo. This realm of the departed spirits seemed in Jewish thinking to have two divisions – a place of bliss, where Lazarus was, and a place of torment, where the Rich man was. Here, the beggar was comforted and the rich man was tormented.
The principles about the after-life in this parable are:
Firstly, there is no extinction or annihilation after death. Both men are conscious.
Secondly, there is no purgatory. Their destination after death is connected with the quality of their earthly lives, 'remember that in your lifetime you received your good things, while Lazarus received bad things.'
Thirdly, since destinations are fixed, transfers are out. 'Between us, a great chasm has been fixed, so that those who want to go from here cannot, nor can anyone cross over from there to us.'
CS Lewis, in his book 'The Great Divorce', makes a strong case that for the Christian, heaven will be an experience which will enhance at a higher level the relationship of faith any Christian had in his everyday life.
Similarly, hell for those who do not believe in Christ as their Saviour, will be a miserable decrease of the worst aspects of their everyday lives.
Fourthly, the haunting appeal of the rich man for a resurrection appearance is rejected. 'I beg you, send Lazarus to my father's house, for I have five brothers....they have Moses and the prophets; let thm listen to them.' The moral witness of Scripture is more effective than a miraculous appearance. We have an insatiable appetite for the spectacular.. They put Jesus to death, and when He rose from the dead, they not only remained unconvinced, they tried to kill off all those who followed Him.

3. TWO MEN IN THEIR DIFFERENCES.

One of the key issues in our consideration of this parable is to attempt to determine why Lazarus the beggar was acceptable to God, and went to the place of bliss after death, and why the rich man went to the place of torment.

Some folk think it boils down to the rich man's callous disregard of the poor man in need at his gate, which is good as far as it goes, but it isn't the whole story.

Others say, simple, because of their wealth, rich people go to hell, and poor people go to heaven, because they have had such a hard time in their earthly life. But wealth is neutral, it's what we do with it that counts, and how far it controls and motivates our actions and fills our dreams. Money is like the guns in the cowboy films – a good servant, but a bad master.
Jesus had rich ladies who used their wealth to support Him. Joseph of Arimathea was a wealthy man who gave his tomb to be used for Jesus' body, and so on...Down the centuries, there have been rich people who have had a simple faith and a generous spirit. One commentator says 'The sin of the rich man is that he has no heart. He thought it was normal that Lazarus should lie in pain and anguish while he wallowed in luxury.'
Some people say 'I am a poor person who has had a hard life, therefore I'll go to heaven' or 'I am a wealthy person, but I've never done anyone any harm, therefore I'll go to heaven.'
Some would say that the sin of the rich man was not that he did wrong things, but that he did nothing.

Another viewpoint is that the rich man went to the place of torment because he was irreligious. But beggars usually go where they will receive some practical support. An orthodox Jew would normally give alms. In the parable, the rich man calls Abraham 'Father', and Abraham calls him 'Son', which indicates that his Jewish religious status was not in question. Referring him to the Law and the Prophets presupposes some knowledge of Jewish teaching and orthodox Jewish belief.

We've already tried to prove that it's not our good works, or lack of them, our wealth, or lack of it, or our religious affiliations, or lack of them, which determines our destination after death.
The only real clue as to why Lazarus was comforted and the Rich Man was tormented is in Lazarus' name. Lazarus is the Greek form of the Hebrew Eleazar, which means 'God is my Helper'. The beggar's simple cry for help to God had found an answer in His deliverance. Psalm 34 verse 6 says 'This poor man cried, and the Lord heard him, and saved him from all his troubles' When Peter tried to walk on the water to Jesus, a long complicated prayer would have sunk him - 'Help, Lord!' was enough.

In the case of little children who die, we can accept what Abraham said in Genesis chapter 18 'Doesn't the Judge of all the earth judge with justice? We can be sure that the sacrifice of Christ on the Cross was effective for babies and little children, and for them as for Christian believers, the principle applies: 'absent from the body, present with the Lord.'

Some people reading this book might be sinking in deep trouble. Others may be worried stiff in case their death would land them in a state of torment. It is not my task to use scare tactics to drive you to Christ. Jesus has been extraordinary in His kindness to us. He humbly chose the Virgin's womb when He came to earth for us. He faced our temptations and died for our sin and rose again on the first Easter Sunday to give us hope after death. Why not cry to Him for help right now?

'Saviour, Saviour, hear my humble cry; and while others You are calling, do not pass me by.'

The real issue lies between you and God.

QUESTIONS

1. Discuss whether you think the story of the Rich Man (Dives) and Lazarus is a real parable. How would you classify it?

2. 'No-one has ever come back to tell us, so how can we know whether there is life after death?' Discuss.

3. Describe the various aspects of contrasting life-style revealed in Jesus' description of these two men.

4. If there is a heaven, how do you think people qualify to get there?

5. Should modern Christians believe in hell? Is this ancient spiteful Teaching inappropriate to post-modernist man?

6. Was Father Abraham unfair in referring the rich man to Scripture Rather than miracle (resurrection) as a basis for faith in God? Discuss

7. Why do you think in this story the rich man went to hell and the poor Man went to heaven?

8. Could you explain what you believe happens to us after we die?

CHAPTER 7

THE CROOKED MANAGER   LUKE 16 v 1-13

Jesus told his disciples: 'There was a rich man whose manager was accused of wasting his possessions. So he called him in and asked him, 'What is this I hear about you? Give an account of your management, because you cannot be manager any longer.'

The manager said to himself, 'What shall I do now? My master is taking away my job. I'm not strong enough to dig, and I'm ashamed to beg – I know what I'll do so that, when I lose my job here, people will welcome me into their houses.'

So he called in each of his master's debtors. He asked the first, 'How much do you owe my master?' 'Eight hundred gallons of olive oil,' he replied. The manager told him, 'Take your bill, sit down quickly, and make it four hundred.'

The he asked the second, 'And how much do you owe?' 'A thousand bushels of wheat,' he replied. He told him, 'Take your bill, and make it eight hundred.'

The master commended the dishonest manager because he had acted shrewdly. For the people of this world are more shrewd in dealing with their own kind than are the people of the light. I tell you, use worldly wealth to gain friends for yourselves, so that when it is gone, you will be welcomed into eternal dwellings.

Whoever can be trusted with very little can also be trusted with much, and whoever is dishonest with very little will also be dishonest with much. So if you have not been trustworthy in handling worldly wealth, who will trust you with true riches? And if you have not been trustworthy with someone else's property, who will give you property of your own?

THE PARABLE OF THE CROOKED MANAGER.

These are stories about ordinary life, which enshrine spiritual principles which are applicable to any culture, so can speak to us today. Our parable in this chapter is found in Luke chapter 16 verses 1-13, and has been called 'The parable of the Unjust Steward', 'The Dishonest Steward', 'The Shrewd Manager', or 'The Story of the Crooked Manager.' Professor William Barclay called it 'A Bad Man's Good Example'.

Here is the parable in Peterson's translation: Jesus said to His disciples, 'There was once a rich man who had a manager. He got reports that the manager had been taking advantage of his position by running up huge personal expenses. So he called him in and said, 'What's this I hear about you? You're fired. And I want a complete audit of your books.' The manager said to himself, 'What am I going to do? I've lost my job as manager. I'm not strong enough to do a labouring job, and I'm too proud to beg....I've got a plan. Here's what I'll do....then when I'm turned out into the street, people will take me into their houses.

'Then he went at it. One after another, he called in the people who were in debt to his master. He said to the first, 'How much do you owe my master?' He replied, 'A hundred jugs of olive oil'
The manager said, 'Here, take your bill, sit down here – quick now- write fifty.'
To the next he said, 'And you, what do you owe?'
He answered, 'A hundred sacks of wheat.'
He said, 'Take your bill, write in eighty.'

Now here's a surprise: the master praised the crooked manager! And why? Because he knew how to look after himself. Streetwise people are smarter in this regard than law-abiding citizens. They are on constant alert, looking for angles, surviving by their wits. I want you to be smart in the same way – but for what is right – using every adversity to stimulate you to creative survival, to concentrate your attention on the bare essentials, so you'll live, really live, and not complacently just get by on good behaviour.'

The context in which this parable is set is interesting. It comes after the Parable of the Lost Son, which is about sinning by wasting money, whereas this parable is about sinning by mismanaging money. Luke chapter 15 tells about someone who squandered money and lost friends, whereas this parable tells us about someone who cunningly managed money and made friends. The Luke 15 parable is about the wickedness of wasteful living, this parable is about the wickedness of fraudulent dealing.

Sometimes Jesus' teaching is startling and a bit scary! Imagine Jesus teaching lessons from the streetwise, Robert Maxwell types! Jesus' hearers were familiar with the astute businessmen, and the hooks crooks and comic singers, who regularly separated them from their hard-earned shekels. It just must have been amazing to hear a Rabbi talking about such things (people are always trying to drive a wedge between the sacred and the secular, so that the

Christian way of doing things and looking at things becomes marginalised, and, they hope, irrelevant).

Of course, the crooked manager in this story belonged to a clan that has not died out. That is why the parables of Jesus have never lost their freshness; they are culturally relevant to every generation. There was an old Scottish legend that once upon a time, there were only two tribes in Scotland – the McGhees and the McTaks. The McGhees were always giving and the McTaks were always taking. The legend said that the McGhees died out and the McTaks took over. The manager in this parable was definitely a McTak...

The McTaks live on! We know of office managers who have had a false set of wage packets to give to their wives. We read about stock market traders, bank employees, and educational heads who have abused their positions to cream off large sums of money. We have heard of sections of industry (notably the building trade) which are prone to be corrupt, of accountants who ask businessmen how much tax they would like to pay, before they do a creative writing exercise on the firm's finances. When I read the parables, I keep thinking of the verse in John's Gospel chapter 2, verses 24 and 25. 'Jesus knew them inside and out, knew how untrustworthy they were. He didn't need any help in seeing right through them.'

The rich owner in this parable may have been an absentee landlord, who had handed over the management of his business interests to someone who was perhaps a clever slave in his employment, but who got so secure in his position that he became a rascal, a bounder, and an embezzler, big-time. The owner's debtors in the story were also rogues, Grade A, Band One. Never an eyebrow was raised when the manager suggested that they falsified their debts for their (and his) benefit.

Perhaps we can be a bit hard on this man Jesus spoke about, who cheated his employer by falsifying his customer's debts for his own benefit. Maybe his is still a common error. Sometimes we have an estimate of ourselves which is above our station in life! Like this manager, we think we are in charge, when we are just employees, tenants rather than owners, stewards of whatever our responsibility is in life. This manager tried to 'live his dream', as the media are encouraging us to do, and it turned into a nightmare. The owner sacked him, and he was facing disaster. He was too puny to labour, and too proud to beg.

In our 'grab it now' society, many of our contemporaries are running into consumer-driven debt, and when things get tough, they are told how easy it is to declare yourself bankrupt...Younger people are particularly vulnerable, and the stuff they think they own might be owned by finance companies. The old idea that you should wait until you can afford it is well and truly out.
Like the manager in Jesus' story, they may have delusions of grandeur.

Life is like a bridge we have to cross. The old spiritual said:
'This world is not my home, I'm just a 'passin' through... We have a temporary and/or sacred stewardship of everything we possess. Some folk have taken unusual views of this responsibility. Andrew Carnegie, who was

not a Christian, said everyone had a responsibility to make as much money as they could, and then to give it away. Fritz Kreisler, the brilliant Austrian-born violinist refused to own a house, claiming this would insult every homeless person in the world. Most people would say their lives are their own. Others have been through major surgery, or have seen poverty in the developing world, or are ex-prisoners of war, and are willing to acknowledge the Fatherhood of God in a general sense, and regard each day as a bonus. Their sense of the stewardship of life covers their intellect, and they try to reach the highest level they can academically. It also covers their health and fitness, because they believe that when they are physically in good shape, this means they will also be in good shape mentally.

People who are in a personal faith-relationship with the Lord Jesus Christ would accept the teaching of the New Testament : 'You are not your own; you have been bought with a price; therefore glorify God in your body, and your spirit, which are His.'

The manager in the story had no such scruples or principles. He got busy winning his customers over by his dishonesty. He encouraged them to falsify their debt figures, and hoped for spin-offs in his favour.

In Jesus' parable of the crooked manager, the owner praised his servant. Why would he do a thing like that? Firstly, he was a planner with an eye to the future, even though he was keen to line his pockets and cushion his fall. At least he thought and planned ahead. We are sometimes caught up in what the philosophers call 'the existential immediacy' of our busy lives. It's as if we're squashed against our neighbours, as if we were on a Tube Train bulleting through the tunnel of life. The manager was in crisis. He had to get off the train, as it were, and think! Jesus' teaching does ring bells, doesn't it? We like to agree with the hymn:
> 'Take from our lives the strain and stress, and let our ordered lives confess the beauty of Thy peace.'

We get caught up in activity, and we buy on impulse, and we can't slow down in any area of our living. Jesus was right. We need to sit down and think and plan ahead, like the manager. Some folk have to get hold of a big piece of paper, and make out three columns: Income, Expenditure, and Where we're going to Cut our Spending. We cannot dream our way out of difficulties. We have to plan our way out.

If you are able to accept the truth of the Bible there is help there. A minister once told me he didn't believe that we had one word that Jesus spoke in the Gospels. But, he said, and I quote : 'The daft old bats I minister to expect me to believe this stuff, so I just speak to them for ten minutes on a Sunday as if it were true.' If you are able to accept that the Gospels contain a true record of what Jesus said, here it is : 'Are you tired? Worn out?....Come to me. Get away with me, and you'll recover your life. I'll show you how to take a real rest. Walk with me and work with me – watch how I do it. Learn the unforced rhythms of grace. I won't lay anything heavy or ill-fitting on you. Keep company with me and you'll learn to live freely and lightly.'

'What am I going to do?' is a good slogan for Christians as well as non-Christians. Christians can act on impulse too. Many a pastor's heart sinks when he hears either of the following fateful phrases: 'We've bought a dog..' or 'We've bought a caravan.' He visualises some energetic young hound trashing an expensive kitchen, so that husband or wife has to skip church to watch the hound on a Sunday morning.

Then the pastor visualises two loungers in the sunshine, far from the madding crowd in church, who are manning the crèche, or teaching a Sunday School class, or putting away chairs or hymn books, or counting the offering. 'What am I going to do?' is a good question for parents too busy to read to their children, or play games with them, and it seems a better option to dump the kids in a soft play area, or plonk them in front of a DVD. We have still to see the long-term effects of these activities, but they can scarcely be called planning ahead. The manager had a plan carefully worked out which he hoped would have good long-term effects.

When we read this parable, it is not only the manager and the dodgy debtors who are as bent as a dog's hind leg. The owner must also be a bit dodgy, approving the manager's dishonest 'mark-down' of goods. Yet he is praised for the energy and awareness he shows in his activities. Jesus said 'streetwise people are smarter in this regard than law-abiding citizens. They are on constant alert, looking for deals, surviving by their wits.' If people spent a tenth of the energy and money on their church as they spent on their cars, their golf or their gardens, how the church would be transformed! A minister in the area where I live, recently said that church-going was a non-contact winter sport. I think he meant that enjoying the summer sunshine was more important to folk than worshipping in church. He probably also meant that when they went to church, folk preferred no contact, so that there would also be no regular commitment to the work of the church. Jesus said 'where your treasure is, there will your heart be also.'

In verse 9 of the parable, Jesus said he wanted His followers to be like the manager. He used his access to cash transactions to build up friendships. We can use our wealth selfishly, or unselfishly, and in so doing, make life easier and sweeter for other folk. A successful car dealer in range of this studio, recently loaned a beautiful, top-of-the- range minibus to some young people who were going to a Christian camp, free of charge.

I was working recently in the lovely Carnegie Library in Dunfermline, the gift of Andrew Carnegie to the citizens of Dunfermline, opened by his mother. Well, after all, he was born in a weaver's cottage there! Like the manager in Jesus' parable, he used 'every adversity to stimulate him to creative survival.' In 1903, James S. Napier, the Glasgow ship-builder, who subscribed to the teaching of Jesus that giving should be secret, gifted the Bethany Hall in Bridgeton to the Glasgow United Evangelistic Association, on condition that his name as donor should not be mentioned in minutes or reports. The friends he made by so doing didn't know until after his death.

The manager was praised for energetic commitment and for using his job and cash crisis as a means of strengthening friendships, so that when he hit serious trouble, the friendships he had made would stand him in good stead.

There is another possible reason why the manager was praised, a lesson we saw elsewhere in Jesus' teaching in the Parable of the Greedy Farmer. The manager's crisis situation forced him to live in the light of the future. Jesus was keen to teach that we should keep a light grip on material things, and be alert to the fact that these things should pass away. The manager was shrewd. He used his present position to win friendships which were like money in the bank to him in the future.

The Bible teaches us to redeem the time, or buy up the opportunities presented to us, because the days are evil, looking forward to the time when we shall stand before Jesus the Judge, to give a report to Him. We will never win our way to heaven by doing good works and helping others. Our righteous acts are too often tainted by our pride. Martin Luther said 'good works do not make a good man, but a good man does good works.' Because our nature is fatally flawed through sin, our only hope is that the righteousness of Jesus will make us fit to appear before God:
> 'Because the sinless Saviour died, my sinful soul is counted free,
> And God the Just is satisfied to look on Him, and pardon me'.

There is only one more lesson from the manager we have time to look at. Jesus extended the story to teach this lesson from the Parable. In Luke chapter 16 verse 10, immediately following the parable, Jesus says:
> 'If you're honest in small things,
> You'll be honest in big things.'

If like this manager you are faithful in your life's responsibilities on earth (the small things), and regard your life as a sacred stewardship, lived out in a relationship of trust in the Lord Jesus Christ, then in the future God can trust you with the true wealth of heaven (the big things).

QUESTIONS

1. Is life a peach or an orange? Is it possible to live our life in segments, church/business, sacred/secular? Discuss. Is the Christian life a holistic, whole-of-life matter, or a part-time interest?

2. Why would you think of this as a daring or risky parable? Have you ever heard a sermon on it?

3. What was there to commend about the manager?

4. Were the owner and the debtors in the parable totally honest? Discuss?

5. What does this parable teach about our stewardship of money and time.?

6. Do we think enough about the future? Is it unhealthy to think and plan for the future? Should Christians take out life insurance?

CHAPTER 8

THE CORRUPT FARM-HANDS   Luke chapter 20 verses 9-19

Jesus went on to tell the people this parable: 'A man planted a vineyard. He rented it to some farmers and went away for a long time. At harvest time he sent a servant to the tenants so they would give him some of the fruit of the vineyard. But the tenants beat him and sent him away empty-handed. He sent another servant, but that one also they beat and treated shamefully and sent away empty-handed. He sent still a third, and they wounded him and threw him out.

Then the owner of the vineyard said, 'What shall I do? I will send my son, whom I love; perhaps they will respect him.'

But when the tenants saw him, they talked the matter over. 'This is the heir,' they said. 'Let's kill him, and the inheritance will be ours.' So they threw him out of the vineyard and killed him.

'What then will the owner of the vineyard do to them? He will come and kill those tenants and give the vineyard to others.'

When the people heard this, they said 'May this never be!'

Jesus looked directly at them and asked, 'Then what is the meaning of that which is written:

'The stone the builders rejected has become the capstone. Everyone who falls on that stone will be broken to pieces, but he on whom it falls will be crushed.'

The teachers of the law and the chief priests looked for a way to arrest Him immediately, because they knew He had spoken this parable against them. But they were afraid of the people.

THE CORRUPT FARM-HANDS

This is possibly the most important parable we shall consider, because of its timing, and its content, and because of the reaction of the religious leaders' reaction to it.. firstly, Jesus told this parable on the third day of Passion Week, in the run-up to the first Easter weekend. Secondly, the focus of the parable's content is on the killing of the son by the crooked farmhands. Thirdly, the parable clearly shows strong reactions by the public, and the religious leaders, who reveal their shock that the nation could be rejected by God, and the clear perception that Jesus told the story against them as killers.

We have said before that the Four Gospels are the most lop-sided biographies ever written. When you read a person's life story, you generally have a well-graded development of the subject – their predecessors, their birth, what they were like as babies and children, their teenage years, into twenties, and so on. The Life of Christ in the Gospels is distinctively different! Two of the four Gospels give some detail about Jesus' birth and infancy, there is nothing about Jesus as a boy, except an incident when He was about twelve years old, nothing about Jesus as a teenager, or about Jesus in His twenties. Luke tells us He was about thirty when He began His ministry as a travelling Rabbi, and then we get a fair amount of information about what happened then, with John's Gospel giving significant and distinctive detail about His ministry in Jerusalem.

When we come to the final Passion Week in His life, the Gospel writers really go to town! – especially Mark. Twenty-seven percent of Mark's Gospel is devoted to Passion Week. The reason for that is as clear as a flying anvil! This is the really important section. Although we are considering the greatest Teacher who ever lived, it is not His teaching which saves us, it is His death and resurrection. The symbol of Christianity is a Cross, not a chalkboard. It is the Cross on the Hill that saves us, not the Sermon on the Mount. The point in relation to this parable is its setting in the middle of the last Passion Week in Jesus' life, on what the old commentator Matthew Henry called 'A day of questions and the Question of the Day.' Read all about it, if you like in Mark chapter 12 or Luke chapter 20. This parable clearly sets out the certainty of Jesus' death as the Son of God, and who would be the agents of His death. The Jewish leaders' mounting hatred of Him reached its climax at this point, because they identified Jesus as the owner's son in the parable, who is killed by the corrupt farmhands. Their secret plans to get rid of Him are exposed in the light of day. The consummate evil of these people erupts , like a boil being lanced, and the drama of world redemption, as Erich Sauer says, unfolds in the Cross and Passion of our Lord.

The whole section including this parable hinges on the issue of **authority. Authority is Debated** in Luke 20 verses 1-8, where there is full frontal questioning of Jesus' authority by the Jewish leaders, and a flurry of wuestions like a deadly serious verbal tennis match. Then **Authority is Depicted** by Jesus in the parable, which is first of all a story of **Responsibility** (the Owner–God, has rights and they are only like tenant farmers with responsibilities). The parable is, secondly, a parable of

Accountability – harvest time has come, and they are accountable. They must produce a share of the grape harvest for the Owner, on time. They fail, and the servants of the Owner return empty-handed. The parable is thirdly a story of **Cruelty,** of the escalating abuse of the Owner's servants by the farmhands. Servants are beaten up and shamefully treated and sent away. In the Old Testament period, the prophet Elijah got some pretty scurvy treatment. In our own times, God's servants overseas are being persecuted while I write. I heard of an African pastor returning from a conference. He had in his possession the offerings taken at the conference. He was set upon, robbed, made to eat his Bible, and then they shot him dead. Jesus' graphic portrayal of their lack of respect for the Owners' servants in this account would possibly trigger great uneasiness, because they prided themselves in their great respect for God. The climax comes in their vicious cruelty they displayed (' Let's kill Him, and the vineyard will be ours.'). The aftermath of the parable shows **Authority Defended,** where Jesus defends the right of God to 'move the goalposts' as it were. The people had seen the main implications of the story as it unfolded (remember this was the Master Teacher they were listening to), and were aghast at the idea that the Owner (God) would 'give the vineyard to others' ie sideline the Jewish nation in favour of others.

The text says 'when the people heard this they said 'May this never be!' In the Greek text this is a strong negative combined with the optative or wishing/desiring mood. 'May this please never come to pass!' or 'Perish the thought!' Jesus comes roaring back with a hard stare – the NIV 'looked directly at them' captures the Greek text – and makes it a double whammy by quoting an Old Testament text 'the stone the builders rejected has become the capstone', defending God's right to reverse proceedings, and backing it up by saying 'everyone who falls on that stone will be broken to pieces, but he on who it falls will be crushed.' Our reaction to Christ is a serious business.

Alex Vidler, in his book 'Christ and Time' makes the Cross of Christ the pivot, focus or fulcrum of world history. All of history, and particularly the salvation-history of the Old Testament, led up to the Cross, anticipating that **'The King will Come.'** The Gospels and Acts tell us that **'The King has Come'**, and the New Testament Letters spell out the implicatins theologically and practically. The Book of Revelation, together with a golden thread of prediction running through the whole Bible tells us that **'The King will Come Again'**. Even the Last Judgement will be conducted in relation to the Cross.

One important feature of this parable is **God's Key Ownership** in relationship to his people, which confirms Old and New Testament teaching. In the eighth century BC, Isaiah the prophet gives the Song of the Vineyard in chapter 5 of the Book of Isaiah. I imagine him like a troubadour, attracting a crowd in some Old Testament equivalent of Ben Jehuda Street in Jerusalem, singing a ballad about his beloved. His song, like Jesus' parable here, centred on a vineyard. He sang about a vineyard on a very fertile hill, and he went to painstaking, back-breaking preparation, so that the vineyard would produce the very best fruit, and it produced only 'wild grapes.' We are in no doubt about identities here either. 'The vineyard of the Lord Almighty is the House of Israel, and the men of Judah are the garden of His delight.' (Isaiah 5 verse

7) No wonder the vine was the image chosen to be stamped on Jewish coinage!   Jesus speaks of Himself as 'the true, the genuine vine, and my Father is the Gardener'.....then He says, 'I am the vine, you are the branches. If a man remains in me and I in him, he will bear much fruit.'

This raises the whole question of our relationship to God. Much religion, even much churchmanship, is whitewash, a superficial, external coating. For some folk, it is like having a vaccination against a disease, to prevent you ever catching the real thing! In this parable, Jesus is telling us that God is like the Owner in the story – He sent His Son, who was killed, and we are implicated. There is no point in blaming the Jews or the Romans for His death. He died for our sins, to bring us into a vital relationship with Him.   Paul Gerhardt, one of the great hymnwriters of the Reformation period, put it like this:

'Extended on a cursed tree, besmeared with dust, and sweat, and blood;
See there, the King of glory see, sinks and expires the Son of God.
Who, who my Saviour this hath done? Who could Thy sacred body wound?
No guilt Thy spotless heart hath known, no guile hath on Thy lips been found.
I, I alone have done the deed; 'tis I Thy sacred flesh have torn;
My sins have caused Thee, Lord, to bleed,
Pointed the nail, and fixed the thorn.'

Jesus' parable of the Corrupt Farmhands must have really upset the religious leaders of His day. It must have been like the scene in the novel 'A Portrait of Dorian Gray', one of the saddest of books, not recommended, but the story is about a fine handsome boy who does a deal that if he lives a wicked life, it should not show in his physical appearance, but on his portrait in the attic. He sinks into unspeakable depravity, and then one day, inevitably, he visits the attic and sees his real self. This parable acted like a mirror held up by Jesus to these people. We dare not live like the wretched Dorian Gray. We are made in God's image and have His likeness about us, no matter how far we have gone away from Him. Jesus wants not only wants to be Lord or Owner of our lives. He has shown us His limitless love by dying on the Cross for us. He wants us to exercise a careful stewardship in our lives, by living for Him every day.

There was once a shoe salesman called Dwight Moody, whose alcoholic father died leaving the family deeply in debt. He went to Chicago, became a Christian, and took two jobs to pay off the family debt. He became involved in Sunday school work and brought children in from the streets of Chicago. Eventually, he became a preacher at city-wide revival meetings. He was deeply involved in the work of the YMCA, and founded several schools for boys and girls, and Bible Colleges like the Moody Bible Institute in Chicago, and the Bible Training Institute in Glasgow. The Tent Hall in Glasgow was founded because of his work. Through his clear and simple preaching, many thousands of people became Christians. Near the end of his life, he was asked what his secret was. He said: 'God had as much of me as there was to give.' There was no good return from the farm hands in this parable. The Jewish leaders they represented failed in their stewardship, We are meant to 'go to school' as the Americans say, on this parable, and live for God.

QUESTIONS.

1. Why do you think the vine was an important symbol for Jews?

2. Who was the Owner of the vineyard meant to represent in Luke 20 Verses 9-19 meant to represent?

3. Why do people reject the idea of God's ownership of their lives? What Rights does God have to expect us to be subject to Him?

4. Can you give any Old Testament examples of the bad treatment God's Servants received?

5. Who does the son in the parable represent? Could you give examples Of the bad treatment he received?

6. See Daniel 3 verses 31-45. How do the themes of Jesus as a rock, or a Stone or a capstone, affect your ideas of Him?

7. How does verse 19 reveal the power of parables?

8. Could you create a modern version of the parable of the Crooked Farmhands which would be roughly equivalent to it?

CHAPTER 9

WHAT IS A MIRACLE?
In this section of the book, we turn from consideration of the parables, to look particularly the miracles of Jesus, based on the world's best-selling book, the Bible, and the four life-stories of Jesus in the Gospels of the New Testament.

Four people were once blindfolded and asked to describe what an elephant was like. One grabbed its tail, and said an elephant was like a rope. The second man put his arms round its leg, and said it was like a tree-trunk. The third man pushed against its side and said it was like a wall. The fourth man felt its trunk and said it was like a drain-pipe. With miracles, as with elephants, it is important to try to grasp the whole picture, and come to a balanced perspective about things.

If you walked past a field and saw a thistle, that wouldn't be a miracle. It wouldn't be a miracle if you walked past a field and saw a cow. If you walked past a field and heard singing, that wouldn't be a miracle. Some folk would think that of you walked past a field and saw a cow sitting on a thistle, singing, that would be a miracle!

Wait a minute – that would be a bit pointless – (except for the points of the thistle on the cow's rear end!). Bible miracles usually have some point or purpose to them. Another factor would be the state of the thistle being sat on by the cow. If the cow sat there in suspended animation on a thistle that hadn't been squashed flat, that would increase your chance of believing that this was a miracle, because normally when a cow sits on a thistle, the thistle would be squashed. Also, cows generally moo, but don't normally sing. This introduces another component to our idea of what constitutes a miracle. Miracles have a supernatural component to them, so that the normal laws of nature seem to be suspended.

Let's move away from pictures of fields, cows thistles and singing, taking with us the two concepts that miracles have a point or purpose, and seem to tamper with the normal laws of nature or science.

We have just written that miracles seem to interfere with the 'normal laws of nature and science'. But what are **they**? Are scientists trying to force us into a rigid polythene strait-jacket of natural law? Remember, scientists have no more to do with the creation of **truth** than clocks have to do with the creation of **time.** They are merely recorders, observers and codifiers of the world around us.

To the Christian believer, the laws of science are the laws of God, who has chosen to place us on space-ship Earth, rotating in a rational universe. We are amazingly just far enough away from the sun not to be cooked, and near enough not to be frozen! There is the wonderful balance of land and water, oxygen and nitrogen, and the amazingly anomalous expansion of water at four degrees Celsius, which prevents the rivers of the world from freezing up in winter...All of this and many more mind-blowing facts make us think that there is a good God at work somewhere...Scientists are merely thinking God's thoughts after Him. Many top scientists have been Christians.

Some Christians have tried to take the heat out of a scientific assault on the Bible's miracle-stories by retreating to a position that there is more than one kind of truth, that religious truth is different from scientific truth. They must think that this is some sort of safeguard for religious truth. But truth is truth whether it comes from the lips of Judas or Jesus, from a smug atheistic scientist or an ordinary convinced Christian. A theory of double truth puts us into the position graphically described by Huxley, where religion and God vanish like the Cheshire Cat in 'Alice in Wonderland' until there is nothing left but the grin...The Biblical evidence should be open to the most rigorous examination, or it ain't worth having, as the Americans would say.

Another factor about the Bible's miracles is that even where you can find a rationalistic or scientific explanation for a miracle, it is the **timing** of it that compels us to retain belief in the event as a miracle. For example, the sequence of the plagues of Egypt can be linked to scientific disruptions to the ecological balance of life in a country so dependent on the river Nile. The plagues can be fitted into some sort of ecological chain reaction. It is the timing of them in the inexorable calendar of God's judgement makes them miraculous. Or else, we can research like mad on the 'dagh gadhol' (big fish) that swallowed Jonah, to discover what species of fish or whale would be able to swallow a man, but the miraculous element is retained when we ask 'why did that big fish happen to be swimming past the ship Jonah was in at that particular minute?' I hope this doesn't confuse you a little more than somewhat...We'll turn our attention to the arguments of one of the strongest and cleverest atheists who ever lived, and a few others who have wriggled out of taking the stories as they stand in the Gospels.

It's healthy to look squarely at any opponent's arguments, and one of the biggest guns that ever fired against Christian miracles was that of David Hume the Scottish philosopher, economist and historian, who lived from 1711 to 1776.

Hume was a brilliant Edinburgh boy who felt, he said, 'an insurmountable aversion to everything but the pursuits of philosophy and general learning.' He set to studying human nature by using the methods of physical science. His faith in reason made him deeply sceptical, and he became the father of modern philosophy. He put his denial of miracles in the form of what he would regard as inescapable logic :

Major Premiss : A miracle is a violation of the laws of nature
Minor Premiss: The laws of nature are unviolable, or unbreakable.
Conclusion: Therefore a rational person is never justified in believing that a miracle ever happened.

As a person locked in a belief system which existed in a closed universe of cause and effect, Hume would say that there must be some other explanation for what seems like a miracle. For example, it seems a miracle because of scientific factors unknown to the writers of the Bible. Or, Hume would say, there were psychological factors which damaged human judgement, like crowd or group hysteria among those who witnessed a so-called miracle. Or, thirdly, the emotional impact of the so-called 'miracle' simply made the healed person feel better. Or, fourthly, Hume would say a behaviour change made it feel like miracle, as when normally selfish people became unselfish under Jesus' direction, so that the narrative of the feeding of the five thousand was merely a 'miracle of sharing.'

Some Christian scholars have taken a non-supernatural approach to the Gospels, so that the miraculous content becomes part of the mythology which has to be stripped away. If you're locked into logic, or are a radical critic of the Bible, then you don't have to try to explain the Bible's, or Jesus' miracle stories.

Some Christians major on miracles, and see them as a vital part of the everyday church. The modern charismatic movement has grown legs, wings and a strong voice since the outpouring of the Holy Spirit at Azusa Street, Los Angeles in 1906, and has fragmented into at least four sub-divisions since. In the 1960s the movement began to permeate most of the major denominations. Just like some kids talk about sex as if they invented it, some charismatics talk about the Holy Spirit as if He were inert before they came on the scene.

Their general claim is that the gifts of the New Testament church are not only available for today's church but an essential part of its everyday life. The dimension of the miraculous is included as central. There have been a few bizarre episodes and emphases, like the claim that gold fillings were miraculously appearing in the mouths of believers, and the Word-Faith movement promoted by people like Paul and Jan Crouch in their $600 million dollar Trinity Broadcasting Network, and Paul Yonggi Cho, Kenneth Copeland, Kenneth Hagin and Benny Hinn. Hagin says 'whatever you say, you get.' The four-stage progression to bring miracles to bear on various aspects of life are: Say it, Do it, Receive it, Tell it. A summary of this kind of teaching is 'Name it and Claim it.' In recent years in Britain the Alpha courses have a charismatic slant, and the Holy Spirit and His gifts are the major emphasis of the course, and feature strongly in the writings of Nicky Gumbel.

When we look at the Bible, we find that God's miraculous activity was sporadic and intermittent rather than daily and constant. The word 'miracle', like the word 'revival', is an overworked word. Miracle stories in the Bible in the main occur in clusters. There are three periods in which these groupings occur - The Exodus Period around the time of Moses, the Prophetic Period around the time of Elijah and Elisha, and the Apostolic Period around the time of Jesus and the Early Church. Each of these was a time of national crisis. The plagues and deliverance have as a motif the challenge of Egyptian religion and the contest between Yahweh and Egypt's gods. The activities of Elijah and Elisha took place in the face of Baal Worship, which Queen Jezebel sought to install as Israel's national faith. In the period of Jesus and the apostles the crisis was the action of Jesus as God incarnate directly in the Gospels and indirectly in the Book of Acts, contrasted with the bankruptcy of Judaism and the threat of Rome. It would be good to look at the special words used in the New Testament to describe miracles.

You may know that the New Testament was originally written in Greek.

1. The first word used for miracles is '**terata**', or 'acts of wonder', that is they inspire awe and wonder. I used to be an examiner for GCSE exams, and I was marking exam papers for teenagers in England who were asked 'What did the disciples say when Jesus stilled the storm on the Sea of Galilee?' One student answered 'Wow'! I was impressed by at the accuracy of this answer...The Greek word focuses on the **WOW** factor. American Gospel song-writers use the word 'awesome' a lot, and this gives the sense of '**terata**'. The word family of the verb '**thaumazo**' = 'to amaze, astonish' belong to the awe and wonder department.

2. Secondly, the miracles are called '**dunameis**', which means 'acts of power'. The Greek word 'dunameis' is the basis for our English words 'dynamite', and 'dynamo'. The miracles of Jesus were **explosive interventions** into the routine of life, as well as the **driving force** behind it.

3. The third word used in the Greek New Testament is '**semeia**', which means 'acts of significance'. This means that the miracles of Jesus are 'signs' pointing to His character as the son of God. John's Gospel uses the word exclusively for Jesus' miracles. After the first sign, the changing of the water into wine at the wedding feast, the writer sums up: 'This, the first of His miraculous signs, Jesus performed at Cana in Galilee. He revealed His glory, and His disciples put their faith in him.' (John 2 verse 11).
In generic terms, the word '**erga**' = 'works' is used in the Gospels both for Christ's miracles and His ordinary deeds of mercy.

The accounts of the healings by Jesus in the Gospels raise particular issues regarding Jesus, His authority, and the people's responses to Him. Keith Warrington comments: 'His ministry of healing was intended to establish truth about Himself rather than act as a healing model for others.' Jesus nowhere suggests that illness has pedagogical value – healing alone has that value. Jesus uses His divine authority in performing miracles to incorporate the outcasts, like the leper, the demon-possessed, or the ritually defiled lady with the haemorrhage, and also to initiate the kingdom.

Official Judaism was spiritually bankrupt and practically powerless in the healing department, although it claimed to be Yahweh's earthly represenatative. . Jesus assumed the role Yahweh had as Healer of His people in the Old Testament period.
At the end of the Gospel, John defines his objectives in writing the Gospel as behaviourally as any College of Education tutor would love to see: 'Jesus did many other miraculous signs... But these are written that you may believe that Jesus is the Christ, the Son of God, and that by believing you may have life through His name.' (John 20 v 30-31).

It is possible to pick out the distinctive features of miracles. They were performed for high, never frivolous reasons. They were performed in several spheres of life – Nature (Luke 5 verses 4-7), People (Mark 1 verses 29-30) and Demons (Mark 5 verses 12-13). They were performed openly before eye-witnesses, and were sometimes performed in spite of lack of faith (John 5 verse 7)

The miracles of Jesus can be classified in two ways, as healing miracles, like healing the crippled man at the Pool of Bethesda, or nature miracles like calming the storm, or feeding the 5000. Ryrie says: 'the question of the possibility of miracles is inseparably connected with the existence of God.' He says Jesus used miracles to demonstrate His deity and to support His validity as Messiah.

For many people, every act of God is a miracle – the birth of a baby, the wonder of a beautiful sunset, the fruit ripening in the summer sunshine – but we are thinking today of special acts which seem to disrupt the normal routine of life or natural law, events which stand as miracles even when we have some rational or scientific explanation for them, because of their timing. In the life of Christ, His miracles were acts of awe-inspiring wonder, demonstrations of His power, or significant acts which pointed to His divine nature. Miracles in the Bible are special **authenticating signs** of God's intervention which were given in times of national crisis, with a definite purpose in view.

Christian people see God at work in two further dimensions we must mention: Providence and Prayer. What many people call 'luck' or 'good fortune' Christians see as God's daily care and organisation of their circumstances. Prayer and Providence open up mini-miracles for those who live in a daily faith relationship with Jesus Christ.

The apostle Paul writes in his letter to the Romans ; 'And we know that in all things God works for the good of those who love Him'. (Romans 8 verse 28) This could be you!

Let me use a personal illustration. When I was a pastor in Edinburgh, members of a group came to see me with a view to gifting a minibus for our Portobello Monday Centre, a meeting place for Alzheimer sufferers. I had forgotten to take their particulars, time was moving on, and I hadn't heard from them. One Wednesday night I prayed that I would get in contact with them soon. The following morning I got on the train from Waverley Station to go to Glasgow to give my lectures, and a man came in and sat opposite me. It was one of the two men who had come to see me! He brought good news about the minibus. So what do YOU think of that? Was it coincidence? There were about half a million other people in Edinburgh who could have sat beside me...I respect your views, but I believe in Providence and Prayer. In the next chapter, we're going to look at how Jesus healed a crippled man.

QUESTIONS

1. Why do people resist the ideas of miracles happening?

2. 'Science tells us that there are no such things as miracles' Discuss

3. Summarise David Hume's arguments against miracles.

4. 'We had a sunny day at the church outing because God answered our Prayers.' 'No, we had a sunny day because there was an anticyclone over the Channel.' Discuss.

5. What is your definition of a miracle?

6. List and explain the main words used for miracles in the Gospels.

7. Why did Jesus perform miracles?

8. Should we expect miracles as a regular feature of church life? Discuss

CHAPTER 10

A PARALYTIC WALKS   Mark 2 verses 1-12

A few days later, when Jesus again entered Capernaum, the people heard that He had come home. So many gathered that there was no room left, not even outside the door, and He preached the word to them. Some men came, bringing to him a paralytic, carried by four of them.

Since they could not get him to Jesus because of the crowd, they made an opening in the roof above Jesus and, after digging through it, lowered the mat the paralysed man was lying on. When Jesus saw their faith, he said to the paralytic, 'Son, your sins are forgiven.'

Now some teachers of the law were sitting there, thinking to themselves, 'Why does this fellow talk like that? He's blaspheming! Who can forgive sins but God alone?'

Immediately Jesus knew in His spirit that this is what they were thinking in their hearts, and He said to them, 'Why are you thinking these things? Which is easier; to say to the paralytic, 'Your sins are forgiven,' or to say, 'Get up, take your mat and walk?' But that you may know that the Son of Man has authority on earth to forgive sins....' He said to the paralytic, 'I tell you, get up, take your mat and go home.'

He got up, took up his mat and walked out in full view of them all. This amazed everyone and they praised God, saying, 'We have never seen anything like this!'

A PARALYTIC WALKS

One of the things we've said is that the miracle stories in the Gospels underline God's interest in people, individually. The God of the Bible is the special champion of the marginalised – the fatherless, the homeless, the widow, the orphan, the refugee. What a good and gracious God we have. That may be an encouragement to you this morning if you are reading this on your own.

God has also a special interest in people in physical need, like the man in our incident today, who was paralysed, and may have been paraplegic, with his paralysis affecting his legs and lower trunk only. Here is 'The Message' translation of the story:

'After a few days, Jesus returned to Capernaum, and word got around that he was back home. A crowd gathered, jamming the entrance so no one could get in or out. He was teaching the Word. They brought a paraplegic to Him, carried by four men. When they weren't able to get in because of the crowd, they removed part of the roof and lowered the paraplegic on his stretcher. Impressed by their bold belief, Jesus said to the paraplegic, 'Son, I forgive your sins.'

Some religious scholars sitting there started whispering among themselves, 'He can't talk that way! That's blasphemy! God and only God, can forgive sins.'

Jesus knew right away what they were thinking, and said, 'Why are you so sceptical? Which is simpler: to say to the paraplegic, 'I forgive your sins,' or say, 'Get up, take up your stretcher, and start walking'? Well, just so it's clear that I'm the Son of Man and authorised to do either, or both.....' (He looked now at the paraplegic), 'Get up. Pick up your stretcher and go home.' And the man did it – got up, grabbed his stretcher, and walked out, with everyone there watching him. They rubbed their eyes, incredulous – and then praised God saying 'We've never seen anything like this!'

Totalitarian states had little time for men like the paralytic in this narrative, who were regarded as a waste of space, were ostracized, or used in degrading medical experiments. Not so with Jesus. We should try to visualise this poor fellow, lying on his mattress, gazing out the window, or window-space. The bold belief mentioned in the narrative must surely include that of the paralysed man as well as his friends. Especially when it came to carrying him on his pallet up the (possibly makeshift) stairs or ladders on to the roof (a flat roof rather than a pitched roof!), then digging through the laminated construction of the roof – beams with leaves and mud plaster layers. The literal translation of the Greek text is: 'they unroofed the roof'! In Israel, the upstairs aliyyah or roof-room was used by the family in the cool evenings. Imagine the commotion the breaking-up of the roof would cause! – bits of falling mud and branches, and through the dust a pallet appears, WITH A BODY ON IT!

In the centre of this commotion, serene and totally in control, is a GREAT PERSON, the Lord Jesus Christ, the Son of Man, who, according to Him has power on earth to forgive sins. When Horace, the Roman playwright, was giving instruction to aspiring young dramatists, he used to say 'Nec deus intersit nisi dignus deo vindice nodus inciderit', which means 'Don't introduce a god unless there is a problem worthy of a god's solution'. Well, here is a problem worthy of a God's solution, and Jesus is just the person to provide it. I said in a previous programme that artists have tended to characterise the Gospel of Mark by the figure of a man, because Jesus is presented there as the Son of Man, the human Christ. 'Son of Man' is Christ's self-chosen title in the Gospels, if you accept their authenticity as they stand. No Gospel writer ever refers to Him by this title, no disciple ever addresses Him by this title.

In using it, Jesus is following normal Hebrew usage to stress His humanity. For example, calling someone a 'son of a murderer' means he is a murderous fellow, a fellow characterised by murderous ideas, so 'Son of Man', means 'truly human person'. Psalm 8 says 'what is man that you are mindful of him, or the son of man that you visit him?' In the prophecy of Ezekiel, the transcendent God frequently addresses Ezekiel the prophet as 'son of man'.

Modern presentations of Jesus sometimes make Him either sub-human or superhuman. In fact He is the only truly authentic, real and genuine human being who ever lived, in the perfection of humanity as God intended it. His personality was untainted with evil, and He faced temptation without falling into evil action as a result of it. Martin Luther's great hymn 'A mighty fortress is our God' refers to the Lord Jesus Christ as 'God's proper man'.
Here is the human Christ in a home, faced with human need, ready to meet it head-on. Isn't it mind-boggling to think that He could come into our homes and hearts today, and meet our need too?

Jesus claimed that He was authorised to heal this man, on earth, in that location.,
We do not only have a Great Person here: we have a **GRUESOME PLACE** here on earth. Our little planet seems an unlikely as well as an unworthy place for miracles to take place. Many millions on our planet live in misery. One child in every three lives in a dwelling with more than five people per room, or with a mud floor. Nearly 20% of the world's children do not have safe water sources or have more than a fifteen-minute walk for water. In South-East Asia alone more than 90, 000,000 children go hungry every day. If an African contracts AIDs, it is virtually a death sentence – 6500 are dying every day, about 1400 of them children. The major cause of the epidemic is unfaithful husbands passing the virus on to their wives.

The poor countries are suffering and the rich countries are miserable. The number of prescriptions for anti-depressant pills in Britain has doubled in the past ten years. The flaunting of 'sexual freedom' in Britain means that in the UK abortion is available for most women - on request. Approximately one in five of all established pregnancies ends in abortion, and more than one in four of all women of childbearing age have had an abortion. What cannot be quantified is the growing groundswell of guilt which women and girls feel because they have had their babies killed. Are we any less decadent than any former civilisations because we consign our unwanted babies to the hospital incinerator instead of the local rubbish dump? The key question is whether a foetus is a blob of jelly or a lump of tissue, which may be extracted or destroyed like teeth, tumours or tonsils rather than a precious life, a little person.

One undisputed fact which emerges from our divorce statistics is that children do not like divorce, and many are in misery because of it. Secular pessimism is rife on both sides of the Atlantic. We live in a world soiled by sin, and trembling before terrorism.

Is there any good news? Yes! People can be changed by God's intervention, here on earth. The miracle story today reveals that our only hope for wholeness lies in Jesus Christ, the Son of Man. The healing of this paraplegic can be a microcosm of God's healing intervention in **our world.** We have turned God's beautiful world into a gruesome place....

Jesus called Himself the Son of Man, who has power on earth to forgive sins. In our discussion of the healing of the paraplegic, we have had quite a lot to say about the Great Person (Jesus) and the Gruesome Place (Earth).

Sometimes physical healing and spiritual salvation seem similar. We have to face the fact of our need for healing. We wouldn't have much time for a doctor who soft-soaped us and understated our physical disease. The Bible says : 'Faithful are the wounds of a friend', and we would want a doctor who told us the truth in his diagnosis of our condition. Years ago there was a Dr Joseph Issels who ran a clinic in Switzerland which specialised in cancer treatment. He subjected his patients to a harsh regime, but achieved a better-than-average success rate. He used to say to them 'Which is more important? That you feel pain? Or that you are getting better? A genuine Gospel comes to us where we are, and is honest with us about our spiritual need, and then points us to the sources of salvation in the Cross and Passion and Resurrection of Jesus. Christians used to sing:
    'Make the Book live to me, O Lord,
    Show me Thyself within Thy Word;
    Show me myself and show me my Saviour
    And make the Book live to me.'

John Bunyan was a Bedfordshire tinker turned preacher who spent about thirteen years in jail because he wouldn't promise not to preach again. While in jail, he wrote a book called 'Pilgrim's Progress', in which he pictures salvation like losing a burden. His Pilgrim is struggling towards the Celestial City with a load on his back. When he comes to the Cross and the Sepulchre, he says:

'Thus far have I come laden with my sin, nor could aught ease the grief that I was in. Must here the burden fall from off my back? Must here the thongs that bound me to it crack? Blest Cross! Blest Sepulchre! Blest rather be the man who there was put to shame for me! Suddenly there was a 'thwack', and his load fell from off his back, and rolled down the far side of the slope. Three

Shining Ones came to him. The first one said 'Your sins are forgiven.' The second one stripped him of his rags and dressed him in a fresh set of clothes. The third one set a mark on his forehead, and gave him a scroll with a seal on it.' That is how Bunyan pictures the radical change that real salvation brings.

In the feverish activity of the home in our narrative today, the paraplegic found healing and radical change – straight strong legs, renewed tissue, strength to walk and carry his mattress. The salvation Christ offers us is a bit like the physical healing he experienced. Apart from God's kindness in Christ we are weak, helpless, polluted and alienated from God by our wicked thoughts and actions. God's work for us through Jesus and in us through the Holy Spirit strengthens us for new life in Him.

The miracle stories raise the whole issue of the authority of Jesus the Miracle-Maker to forgive sin, like He says in Mark 2 v 12, or Luke 5 v 24. It also raises the issue of the exclusive claims of the Christian Gospel, that there is one God and one Mediator between God and man, the man Christ Jesus. Joseph Hart's hymn says:
'Come ye sinners, poor and needy, weak and wounded, sick and sore,
Jesus ready stands to save you, full of pity, love and power:
He is able, he is willing, doubt no more...
Lo the Incarnate God ascended pleads the merit of His blood,
Venture on Him, venture fully, let no other trust intrude;
None but Jesus, none but Jesus
Can do helpless sinners good.'

Jesus isn't like one of those quack doctors who travelled in the Wild West, hawking their vile-tasting medicines or weird cures. He alone can prescribe the right medicine for our soul's diseases. This Gospel story displays His sureness of touch in dealing with individuals. Pastors and priests and other human agents can offer us limited help, but only Jesus can forgive our sins. He has unique qualifications to do this for us. The writer to the Hebrews puts it like this: Now that we know what we have – Jesus, this great High Priest with ready access to God – let's not let it slip through our fingers. We don't have a priest who is out of touch with reality. He's been through weakness and testing. Experienced it all – all but the sin. So let's walk right up to Him and get what He is so ready to give. Take the mercy, accept the help....while he lived on earth, anticipating death, Jesus cried out in pain, and wept in sorrow as He offered up priestly prayers to God. Because He honoured God, God answered Him... Then, having arrived at the full stature of His maturity and having been announced by God as High Priest... He became the source of eternal salvation to all who believingly obey Him.' I couldn't put it better myself!

The paraplegic in the incident we're considering was able to stand up, grab his mattress, and walk out of the home he was in. The spectators were gob-smacked, to say the least. They rubbed their eyes, incredulous – then praised God saying 'We've never seen anything like this!'

The story highlights a Great Person and a Gruesome Place, but it also highlights a Glorious Pardon. The healing that took place was total, and instantaneous. No more grubbing about in bed all day, no more dependency culture for this fellow. Jesus set him on his way, totally and radically changed. That is the way of Jesus. I could take you to many people who have experienced this change. I know a local lady who took in ironing. I called her 'The Iron Lady'! She was an alcoholic failure for eighteen years, and tried to take her own life many times. She trusted in Jesus the Saviour, and her life was revolutionised. One Christmas years after her life was changed, she was surprised to find her daughter, who had visited her at Christmas, crying beside the fire. When she asked her daughter what was wrong, the daughter said she had just remembered one Christmas when she had visited – the house was like a tip, frozen cold, her mother had only some mouldy bread in the house, and was shuffling around the place,drunk, in her dressing gown, with her hair in a mess. Now it was spotless, the larder was full, mother was wearing a lovely dress, and the house was beautifully warm. Her Mum was a happy person with a new life.

A Glasgow man whose life had been changed said 'A'm happier noo when ah'm no happy than ah wis when ah wis happy before!' Which being translated is 'I'm happier now when I'm not happy than I was when I used to be when I was happy!'

John Masefield, a former Poet Laureate, wrote 'The Everlasting Mercy' in 1911. He tells the story of how the evil Saul Kane is convicted by the words of a Salvation Army girl, and his life is transformed:

'O glory of the lighted mind, how dead I'd been, how dumb, how blind.
The station brook, to my new eyes was babbling out of Paradise.
The waters rushing from the rain were singing Christ was risen again,
I thought all earthly creatures knelt, from rapture of the joy I felt.
The narrow station-wall's brick ledge the wild hop withering in the hedge,
The lights in huntsman's upper storey were parts of an eternal glory
Were God's eternal garden flowers.
I stood in bliss at this for hours.'

The joy of the Lord's pardon has been a strengthening force in many lives. A profligate Cornish tin-miner called Billy Bray believed in Christ, and experienced the spiritual equivalent of the paraplegic's healing. In his biography, entitled 'The King's Son', Billy Bray is quoted: 'In an instant, the Lord made me so happy that I cannot express what I felt. I shouted for joy. I praised God for what He had done for a poor sinner like me. I think this was November 1823...I remember this, that everything looked new to me, the people, the fields, the cattle, the trees. I was like a new man in a new world....Some said I was mad; and others that they would get me back next pay-day. But, praise the Lord, it is now more than forty years ago, and they have not got me yet. They said I was a mad-man, but they meant I was a glad-man, and, glory be to God, I have been glad ever since.' Such is the Glorious Pardon you and I can know today.

QUESTIONS.

1. 'All disease is of the devil, and is part of our fallen world.' Discuss

2. See Mark 2 verse 5. Is the faith of the paralysed man included in the phrase 'their faith'? Do you believe in proxy faith, that is, the four men exercised faith on behalf of their friend?

3. Is there any connection between sin and illness, or between forgiveness and healing?

4. The issue of authority is important here. What does Jesus say about who has authority to forgive? Discuss.

5. See Daniel 7 verse 13, Ezekiel 2verse 1 and Mark 2 verse 10, 10 verse 45, and 14 verse 62. Why does Jesus use this title 'Son of Man' so much in the Gospels? Discuss.

CHAPTER 11

THE MAN AT THE POOL.   John chapter 5 verses 1 – 15.

Some time later, Jesus went up to Jerusalem for a feast of the Jews.

Now there is in Jerusalem near the Sheep Gate a pool, which in Aramaic is called Bethesda and which is surrounded by five covered colonnades. Here a great number of disabled people used to lie - the blind, the lame, the paralysed. One was there who had been an invalid for thirty-eight years. When Jesus saw him lying there and learned that he had been in this condition for a long time, He asked him, 'Do you want to get well?'

'Sir,' the invalid replied, 'I have no-one to help me into the pool when the water is stirred.   While I am trying to get in, someone else goes down ahead of me.'

Then Jesus said to him, 'Get up! Pick up your mat and walk.' At once the man was cured; he picked up his mat and walked.

The day on which this took place was a Sabbath, and so the Jews said to the man who had been healed, 'It is the Sabbath; the law forbids you to carry your mat.' But he replied, The man who made me well said to me, 'Pick up your mat and walk.'

So they asked him, 'Who is this fellow who told you to pick it up and walk?' The man who was healed had no idea who it was, for Jesus had slipped away into the crowd that was there.

Later Jesus found him at the Temple and said to him, 'See, you are well again. Stop sinning, or something worse may happen to you.' The man went away and told the Jews it was Jesus who had made him well.

THE MAN AT THE POOL.

Earlier, we asked the question 'What is a Miracle?', and tried to dismiss any frivolous ideas of miracles as tricks, and look at them through a Biblical viewer. They are special, purposeful acts which seem to break the laws of nature and science, but even where we can find a naturalistic explanation, the timing element retains the miraculous flavour. Miracles in the Bible occur in clusters at times of religious and national crisis, and the three main words in the Greek New Testament indicate that they are acts of wonder, acts of power and acts of significance. As far as the Gospels' account of Jesus' life is concerned, they are self-authenticating acts which prove His deity and inspire faith in His followers. All the miracles in John's Gospel are called 'signs'. The Gospels contain both nature miracles, like feeding the five thousand, and healing miracles, like the incident we are going to look at today – the healing of the blind man at the pool of Bethesda in Jerusalem. This miracle story is found in John's Gospel chapter 5. Here it is in from Peterson's 'The Message':

'Soon another Feast came around and Jesus was back in Jerusalem. Near the Sheep Gate in Jerusalem there was a pool, in Hebrew called Bethesda, with five alcoves. Hundreds of sick people – blind, crippled, paralyzed – were in these alcoves. One man had been an invalid there for thirty-eight years. When Jesus saw him stretched out by the pool and knew how long he had been there, he said 'Do you want to get well?'

The sick man said, 'Sir when the water is stirred, I don't have anybody to put me in the pool. By the time I get there, somebody else is already in.'

Jesus said, 'Get up, take your bedroll, start walking.' The man was healed on the spot. He picked up his bedroll and walked off.

That day happened to be the Sabbath. The Jews stopped the healed man and said, 'It's the Sabbath. You can't carry your bedroll around. It's against the rules.'

But he told them, 'the man who made me well told me to. He said, 'Take your bedroll and start walking.'

They asked, 'Who gave you the order to take it up and start walking?' But the healed man didn't know, for Jesus had slipped away into the crowd.

A little later, Jesus found him in the Temple and said, 'You look wonderful ! You're well! Don't return to a sinning life or something worse might happen .'

The man went back and told the Jews that it was Jesus who had made him well. That is why the Jews were out to get Jesus – because He did this sort of thing on the Sabbath.

But Jesus defended himself. 'My Father is working straight through, even on the Sabbath. So am I.'

That really set them off. The Jews were now not only out to expose Him, they were out to kill Him. Not only was He breaking the Sabbath, but He was calling God his own Father, putting himself on a level with God.'

Each of the four Gospel writers have their own viewpoint, and this miracle story appears only in John's Gospel. In art and sculpture down the centuries, the Gospel writers are given a different visual 'password'. Matthew is presented as a lion, because he pictures Jesus as the Lion of the Tribe of Judah, fulfilling Old Testament prophecies. Mark is depicted as a man, because in that Gospel Jesus is presented as 'The Son of Man', who came to give His life a ransom for many, as He said in Mark chapter 10 verse 45. Luke is sometimes painted as a lamb, or sometimes an ox, because in Luke's Gospel Jesus is the Servant of God, and these two beasts are creatures of service. The artists have often represented John as an eagle, the soaring creature of panoramic vision, because that is the nearest to John's perceptive description of Jesus as the eternal Logos, the Word who became flesh and 'camped among us', the 'one and only Son of the Father, full of grace and truth, who became the travelling teacher of Galilee and Jerusalem.

There is a dramatic dimension to John which is not present in the other Gospels. John's great Prologue pictures Jesus the Logos as living eternally with God the Father, closely involved in the creation of the universe, and as the light which shines on in the darkness, and has never been snuffed out. The hinge passage in John Chapter 1 comes in verse 14 'And the Word became flesh and made His dwelling among us. We have seen His glory, the glory of the One and Only, who came from the Father, full of grace and truth.' The action then unfolds, introducing us to John the Baptizer, and the first disciples or followers of Jesus.

It is as if John has let the readers into a secret, which will help them to understand Jesus' divine background, so that they will come to believe in Him. Shakespeare uses the same sort of dramatic technique in his soliloquies, when the action about to unfold is anticipated in a speech given in advance by a lone actor.

The nearest parallel in the Bible to the prologue in John's Gospel is in the Old Testament book of Job. There the reader is allowed in the first two chapters to have a peep into the heavenly court, where Satan reports to God, and responds to God's taunt about what a good guy Job is by obtaining permission to tempt him and make him suffer. The discussion of suffering which follows has this heavenly background, and the reader is in on the secret. So it is with John's Gospel, and the 'acts of significance' (the miracles in John are all called 'signs') are meant to be signposts to the reader who has prior knowledge of Jesus' heavenly credentials. Now we break off for some music.)

There are various ways of looking at John's Gospel. We can use what are called the 'I AM' sayings as pegs on which to hang our understanding. In these sayings, Jesus is making certain claims about Himself, like 'I am the Bread of Life', 'I am the Good Shepherd', 'I am the Way, the Truth and the Life', 'I am the Resurrection and the Life,' 'I am the Vine', and so on. This is one good way of studying the Gospel. Another way is to use the miracle stories, like the incident of the crippled man at the Pool of Bethesda, as focal points of interest. As I said before, there are three main words for miracle in the Gospels : terata which are acts of wonder, dunameis, which are acts of power, and the word used exclusively in John, semeia, which are acts of significance. Another way of looking at the Gospel is to think of it as a series of 'people who met Jesus and were never the same again'. The Gospel is full of personal incidents of this kind – Nathaniel, Nicodemus, the Woman of Sychar, The man at the Pool, the man born blind, Lazarus, and so on. They are there to show us that God is interested in individuals. Abraham Lincoln said that God must have loved ordinary people – He made so many of them, and that means you and me this morning...Marxist philosophy majors on the masses; the Gospels major on individuals.

The Marxist finds fulfilment in sacrificing his life for the greater good of those who follow him. The Christian finds fulfilment in giving his life to God through faith in Jesus Christ, and finding eternal life as quality living here and now as well as then and there. Marxist philosophy majors on bread for the masses; Jesus and His followers say man shall not live by bread alone, but by dependence on God's Word. Marxism focuses on the material. Christians believe that what is seen is temporary, but what is unseen is eternal. It is therefore easy to understand the growth of opposition to Jesus, as we read through John chapters 5-8, as Jesus faced critics entrenched in privilege, who looked down on the people of the land as they called them, and had forgotten that they were meant to be a saving remnant for God, but many of whom were happy to preen themselves as a saved remnant, believing that God made the non-Jewish nations to be fit only to serve as fuel for the fires of hell. They had forgotten that the God of the Old Testament was the special champion of the poor, and the underprivileged, like the man in our story.

Scholars used to deny that there was a place called the Pool of Bethesda (there are variants of the name), with its five alcoves, but renovations near St Anne's church, by the Sheep Gate in north-east Jerusalem, uncovered what was possibly this important site.

The opening verses of the chapter reveal that the man beside the Pool of Bethesda lived a Life without Hope, like so many people in the world today. Each sunrise brings them, like this man, a hopeful trail which peters off into a hopeless treadmill. He was one of the long-term sick, with no means of obtaining the resources to make him well. He knew something of the temporary and spasmodic nature of this healing spa water of Bethesda. He did have friends who brought him there every day for many years, but he lost in the cut-throat rat-race to get to the pool while it was bubbling. When the water subsided, he was back in the pit of his misery. In January 2006 I visited an African in his little house in Kenya, lying in his underpants on a thin mat on his living-room floor, very ill. The family could not afford to pay to take him to hospital, and he died two weeks after I saw him. Many children in the developing world do not have the nourishment for their bodies and brains to grow, and are disadvantaged from birth. Debilitating diseases like dysentery are easily cured, but few bother.

There may be some people reading for whom a broken marriage full of recrimination and bitter memories, or a growing mountain of debt, bring you a life without hope, like the man in the story. You feel like a hopeless hamster imprisoned on a wheel, and cannot see a way out. In this miracle story in John chapter 5, Jesus heard about this invalid who had been coming to the Pool for thirty-eight years, He went alongside him, and spoke kindly to him. The world is dying for a smidgeon of love, and Jesus can come alongside you or me today, and speak kindly to us. Cry out to Him...you can find deliverance and the friendship of the Friend of Sinners. Fun and Treats are amazingly unsatisfying, and can leave a sour taste and an empty heart with a space which only God can fill..

Augustine said that God made us for Himself, and our hearts are restless until they find their rest in God.

There's an old hymn which says :
'The Saviour can satisfy fully the heart which this world cannot fill,
His presence can sanctify wholly the heart that is yielded and still;
The Saviour can solve every problem, the tangles of life can undo,
There is nothing too hard for Jesus, there is nothing that He cannot do.'

Jesus went to the invalid at the Pool of Bethesda in Jerusalem, and asked him what many folk would regard as the most stupid question imaginable: 'Do you want to get well?' Hey Jesus, are you kidding? 'I've been coming here for thirty-eight years to get healed!' 'Do you think I just come here for the good of my health?' I want a life apart from ill-health.' The actual text (John 5 v7) tells us the man says to Jesus, 'Sir, I have no one to help me into the pool...' The invalid who had a life without Hope had also a life without Help. Perhaps you feel like that as you read this. You bottle up your problems, and suppress your sins because you feel utterly alone. You feel that if you opened up to someone, they would recoil and withdraw, quickly. Sometimes, like the invalid in the story, you feel some comfort in being near to help, but it never comes for you.

There may be something else. The question Jesus asked was not so daft as some folk would say. There is such a thing as 'institutional inertia', where people actually enjoy their condition of disadvantage, and seeing others buzzing around to help. How many times today do we read of the carer dying before the patient. Years ago I used to visit an elderly couple. The wife was housebound, and the husband always made a fuss of any visitors. He cared for his wife, cleaned the house shopped and cooked and gardened, and was always on the go. He took a heart attack one day and died, and guess what ? The Sunday after the funeral the wife appeared at church for the first time for years, and attended regularly for years afterwards.

The same sort of thing can happen in hospitals...Some people enjoy bad health. So Jesus asked a good question: 'Do you want to get well?'. The first step towards wholeness is a deep desire for it. One commentator says: 'an eastern beggar often loses a good living by being cured.' The man's life in this story was a study in tragedy before Jesus came, and Jesus' question reveals a search for honesty. In the 1960s the Bishop of Woolwich wrote a book called 'Honest to God', and that's what we have to be if we want to experience the miracle of Christ's healing and deliverance. John tells us in chapter 2 verse 24 and 25 'Jesus knew all men. He did not need man's testimony about man, for He knew what was in a man. The hymn says:
'O Saviour Christ, Thou too art man, Thou too wast tested, tempted, tried, Thy kind but searching glance can scan the very wounds that shame would hide.'

Jesus healed the Man at the Pool – no messing about, no fancy stuff, no gradual or partial healing. The text says: 'Jesus said to him 'Get up! Pick up your mat and walk.' At once the man was cured; he picked up his mat and walked.
There is an interesting sideline here in the text. The healed invalid refers to Jesus as 'the man who made me well', and verse 13 says 'the man who was healed had no idea who it was, for Jesus had slipped away into the crowd that was there.' Jesus had performed a stupendous miracle, and then slipped away into the crowd. There is the greatest possible contrast between the guys we sometimes see on television with the white suits, golden knuckledusters and podgy white hands which have never done a day's work, and the Lord Jesus Christ. Ostentation was out for Jesus. There was no whooping and hollering, no unseemly showmanship, no extravagant claims. The strong hands of the Carpenter fixed this man's broken life.

Sometimes Jesus is called 'The Great Physician'. Lawyers usually see people at their worst, and pastors usually see people at their best, but doctors, it is said, see us as we really are. Jesus saw this invalid as he really was, and he would never be the same again. The man who had a Life without Hope and a Life without Help, now embarked on a Life without Hindrance.

It wasn't an easy life. He was immediately plunged into criticism, because Jesus healed this man on the Sabbath Day, the rules of which the Jews had woven into a strangulating strait-jacket. Their pundits argued out whether you could eat an egg laid on the Sabbath (you couldn't, because little henny had to work, and Sabbath working was forbidden). Or whether you could put ointment and a bandage on a cut on the Sabbath (you could put a bandage but no ointment, because it would be working to heal the cut). And so on. Later Jesus identified Himself to the man in his new-found freedom, interestingly at the Temple. The work of Jesus in our lives prompts us to worship God, and our life becomes a long hymn of gratitude.

Jesus was absolutely honest with the man and says: 'See, you are well again. Stop sinning, or worse may happen to you.' Physical healing was no guarantee of spiritual healing. Jesus obviously knew something about the man's past, and calls him to 'lay aside every sin' as the Letter to the Hebrews tells us. To repent of our sin and trust in the given life and shed blood of Christ as our means of deliverance implies a change in lifestyle. Children in Sunday-School used to sing :

> 'Twas a grand day when I was born again, 'twas a grand day when I was born again, 'twas a grand day when I was born again, 'twas a grand day when I was born again.....The sins I used to do I do them no more, the sins I used to do I do them no more, the sins I used to do I do them no more, 'twas a grand day when I was born again'

QUESTIONS

1. What does John 5 verse 5 tell us about Jesus' relations with the crowd with respect to the invalid?

2. Was it a silly or irrelevant question in verse 6 : 'Do you want to get well?'

3. Are there people who 'enjoy bad health'? Can you give any examples from your experience?

4. See verse 7. Do you believe in 'healing waters'? What do you think happened at this pool (see marginal footnote in the text). Does it have a bearing on this incident?

5. Why were the Jewish authorities upset? Was it simply a question of Sabbath observance?

6. Is there a Sabbath/Sunday link-up? Should we keep Sunday special? What are the advantages/disadvantages?

7. Comment on verse 13 in the light of present-day faith healers.

8. What do you think Jesus meant by His warning in verse 14? Discuss whether it produced a bad reaction by the cured invalid.

CHAPTER 12

THE CROWD ON THE HILL.   John Chapter 6 verses 1-15, 25-35.

Some time after this, Jesus crossed to the far shore of the Sea of Galilee, (that is, the Sea of Tiberias), and a great crowd of people followed Him because they saw the miraculous signs He had performed on the sick. Then Jesus went up on a mountainside and sat down with His disciples. The Jewish Passover Feast was near.

When Jesus looked up and saw a great crowd coming toward Him, He said to Philip, 'Where shall we buy bread for these people to eat?' He asked this only to test him, for He already had in mind what He was going to do. Philip answered Him, 'Eight months wages could not buy enough bread for each one to have a bite!'

Another of His disciples, Andrew, Simon Peter's brother, spoke up. 'Here is a boy with five small barley loaves and two small fish, but how far will they go among so many?'

Jesus said, 'Have the people sit down.' There was plenty of grass in that place, and the men sat down, about five thousand of them. Jesus then took the loaves, gave thanks, and distributed to those who were seated as much as they wanted. He did the same with the fish.

When they had all had enough to eat, He said to His disciples, 'Gather the pieces that are left over. Let nothing be wasted.' So they gathered them and filled twelve baskets with the pieces of the five barley loaves left over by those who had eaten.

After the people saw the miraculous sign that Jesus did, they began to say, 'Surely this is the Prophet who is to come into the world.' Jesus, knowing that they intended to come and make Him king by force, withdrew again to a mountain by Himself...

When they found Him on the other side of the lake, they asked Him, 'Rabbi, when did you get here?'

Jesus answered, 'I tell you the truth, you are looking for me, not because you saw miraculous signs but because you ate the loaves and had your fill. Do not work for food that spoils, but for food that endures to eternal life, which the Son of Man will give you. On Him God the Father has placed His seal of approval.'
Then they asked Him, 'What must we do to do the works God requires?'
Jesus answered. 'The work of God is this; to believe in the One whom He has sent.'
So they asked Him, 'What miraculous sign will you give that we may see it, and believe You? What will you do? Our forefathers ate the manna in the desert; as it is written: 'He gave them bread from heaven to eat.'

Jesus said to them, 'I tell you the truth, it is not Moses who has given you the bread from heaven, but it is my Father who gives you the true bread from heaven. For the bread of God is He who comes down from heaven and gives life to the world.'

'Sir,' they said, 'from now on give us this bread.'

Then Jesus declared, 'I am the bread of life. He who comes to me will never grow hungry, and he who believes in me will never be thirsty.'

THE CROWD ON THE HILL

The miracle under consideration in this chapter must be very important. A version of it appears in every one of the four Gospels, and that only happens with one other event – the Resurrection, so we'll be rewarded for giving it good attention.

The setting of it was a hill on the shores of the Sea of Galilee, or the Sea of Tiberias, or Chinnereth ('the harp-shaped' Sea). It was probably towards the Golan Heights area east of the Sea, and the term 'the hillside' may mean it was a familiar rendezvous. Jesus and His disciples were both needing a rest, but as usual, He responded to the needy crowd, who were 'like sheep without a shepherd.' The miracle evokes discussion with the religious leaders, and the punchline of the passage is Jesus' astounding claim to be the Bread of Life, but here is part of the narrative in Peterson's version:

'After this, Jesus went across the Sea of Galilee (some call it Tiberias). A huge crowd followed Him, attracted by the miracles they had seen Him do among the sick. When He got to the other side, He climbed a hill and sat down, surrounded by His disciples. It was nearly time for the Feast of Passover, kept annually by the Jews.

When Jesus looked out and saw that a large crowd had arrived, He said to Philip, 'Where can we buy bread to feed these people?' He said this to stretch Philip's faith. He already knew what He was going to do.
Philip answered, 'Two hundred silver pieces wouldn't be enough to buy bread for each person to get a piece.'

One of the disciples – it was Andrew, brother to Simon Peter – said, 'There's a little boy here who has five barley loaves and two fish. But that's a drop in the bucket for a crowd like this.'

Jesus said, 'Make the people sit down.' There was a nice carpet of green grass in this place. They sat down, about five thousand of them. Then Jesus took the bread and, and having given thanks, gave it to those who were seated. He did the same with the fish. All ate as much as they wanted. When the people had eaten their fill, he said to His disciples, 'Gather the leftovers so nothing is wasted.' They went to work, and filled twelve large baskets from the leftovers from the five barley loaves. John 6 verse 35 says 'Then Jesus declared, 'I am the Bread of Life. He who comes to me will never go hungry, and he who believes in me will never be thirsty.'

Many people are sceptical about this miracle, partly because of its sheer extravagance. Professor William Barclay regarded it as a miracle of communal sharing rather than a miracle of divine provision. He claimed that the crowd were prompted to share their packed lunches with each other, so that the naturally selfish were inspired to be unselfish for a change. I am sure there was more to it than that. Although in strict classification this would go down as a nature miracle rather than a healing miracle, the influence of the events of that day would be fixed in the hearts and lives of those who were there until their dying day.

The miracle is also an illustration of the measureless compassion of the Lord Jesus Christ. He was moved by the plight of the crowd, not only because they were like sheep without a shepherd, but because they were harassed and hungry. Every time we read in the Gospels that Jesus was moved with compassion, it meant that He had a deep physical response which prompted Him to take some action. The Greek verb 'splangchnizomai' includes the 'splangchna', or viscera, meaning he had what we could call a 'gut reaction' to human need. He would then speak to the crowd, or heal the leper or feed the multitude as He did here.

The physical details of the story showed that there was more than enough for everyone who was there, but there was no extravagant waste. The disciples collected up the left-overs, and would have stale bread to eat for the next day or two.

Bread is a vital commodity in the history of the world. Communist dogma makes too much of it, as Jesus said in the Temptation narrative: 'Man shall not live by bread alone, but by every word that comes from the mouth of God.' There is more to being a man than being a bread-producing labour unit. We mustn't forget the spiritual dimension of life. One of the key reasons behind the French Revolution in 1789 was the escalating price of bread. If you have ever been to France, you will become aware of the importance of bread to a Frenchman from day one. Similarly, the increasing price of bread was a main factor behind the Russian Revolution in 1917, and the Polish Revolution under the electrician Lech Walesa at the Gdansk shipyards in 1980.

Jesus' 'I AM' saying in this chapter deserves particular attention. It isn't simply one of the pegs on which John hangs his account of the Lord Jesus Christ, the Logos who became flesh, but is a fresh advance in the self-disclosure of Jesus as Saviour. 'I am the Bread of life. He who comes to me will never go hungry, and he who believes in me will never go thirsty.'

CC Ryrie gives a tightly-knit analysis of this narrative. Firstly, he highlights Jesus' **faithfulness in teaching**. Jesus was **weary** (the tenses in verse 2 indicate continuous following), but He was **willing** to minister in spite of His tiredness, and this involved **working**, because teaching, a physically draining activity, was a prominent part of His ministry. Then Ryrie pinpoints Jesus' **faithfulness in training**, and notes **the inquiry of the Lord** (where to buy bread?), and the **importance of the leaders** (Philip and Andrew brought the boy forward). Thirdly, he stresses Jesus' **faithfulness in tending**, in relation to the supply, the seating the serving and the satisfying!

To the less organised and simpler believer, there are three features of true Christianity encapsulated in this verse:

1. PRESENT TENSE CHRISTIANITY: 'I AM'
When Jesus uttered these 'I am' sayings in the fourth Gospel, He was assuming totally the role which God the Father had as YAHWEH in Old Testament times. This supports to some extent the idea some scholars have of the 'Messianic Secret', because not everyone would make the connection

between, for example, John chapter 6 and Exodus chapter 3, which marked a stage in the development of God's self-revelation to Moses in the Old Testament.

Scholars have spilt much ink attempting to explain the meaning of the name Yahweh. The consensus is that it is some part of the verb 'to be' in Hebrew, probably the causative mode. Therefore it can be a Creation Name – 'the One who causes to be what comes into existence', or it could be a Crisis Name – the One who Is, or Will be, our Helper in any emergency situation, or it could be a Covenant Name - the One whose consistency and integrity we can count on an trust in down the generations.

The Lord Jesus fulfils all these roles under the New Testament era. He is the same yesterday, and today and forever, and those who trust in Him are like sailors who lash themselves to a fixed point for security in a storm.

Some people are escapees from the present. One of my friends has to leave the room when the six o'clock news comes on. He is taken up with the distant past (the period of the Greeks and the Romans), or the recent past (the gangster era of the twenties and thirties), or the distant future (he reads a lot of science fiction, and is a 'Trekkie'). No matter how bad the times are, Jesus is saying to us 'I am' with you in that situation.

2. BASIC LEVEL CHRISTIANITY: 'THE BREAD OF LIFE'

In this part of the saying, Jesus is assuring us not only of his presence, but of His provision for us at the deepest level. In the eighth century BC, the prophet Isaiah, and the nation of Judah were facing uncertain times. The menacing shadow of Assyria loomed over the land. The covenant people of the Kingdom of Judah had wandered far away from God. In Isaiah 1 verse 18, God called them to respond: 'Come now, let us reason together,' says the LORD. 'Though your sins are like scarlet, they shall be as white as snow; though they are red as crimson, they shall be as wool.' We are made in God's image, after His likeness, with the dignity of His deity about us. We have the rationality to respond to Him at the deepest level. And at the deepest level, through the work of Christ on the Cross, he can deal with our sins by cleansing us and forgiving us and renewing us. Similarly, Jesus the Bread of life comes at the deepest level to nourish our spiritual appetites, and satisfy our souls.

3. FACE TO FACE CHRISTIANITY: 'HE WHO COMES TO ME WILL NEVER GO HUNGRY, AND HE WHO BELIEVES IN ME WILL NEVER GO THIRSTY.'

There are widely varying views of religion. Karl Marx thought it was the opiate of the people, a kind of tranquiliser to keep us supine and obedient. The Darwinians think it is an evolutionary hangover. The Freudians think God is a frustrated father complex. One of my pupils defined religion as the pillow on which we rest our doubts. But to the Christian, religion is a face-to-face matter, a relationship between an individual and a Being believed to be God, which results in a commitment of faith, acts of devotion, and a life of service. In Jesus' language, it is 'he....me, he ....me' Scripture Union had a publication called 'Jam' which stood for 'Jesus and Me'.

The relationship is not only personal, it s dynamic, involving verbs, which any schoolboy used to be able to tell you, are 'doing words'. That is why Jesus talks about 'he who comes….he who believes…' Christianity is a dynamic relationship which involves movement from us to Christ. The verb to believe is to move outside of our comfort zone to where Jesus calls us. Someone said to me recently that we should spell faith 'R-I-S-K'. Sometimes in the New Testament, the verb 'to believe' is combined with a preposition of motion, or a dative case, so that we believe towards Jesus, or upon Jesus. Belief is the central feature of the faith that takes us from our self-sufficiency to Christ's great work of dying for our sins, of yielding His body, and shedding His blood on the Cross. It's as straightforward as ABC. The Good News gives us something to Accept (that we are sinners) something to Believe (that Christ died for our sins) and something to Confess (that we have trusted Him and belong to Him).

The scene on the hillside was a stupendous one. In Mark's version of it in his Gospel, he remembered the green grass (a seasonal thing), and the people sitting down, literally 'garden beds, garden beds', colourful and organised. Many of those who were there that day would have changed lives for ever.

QUESTIONS

1. In China, they used to have what they called 'Rice Christians', because they wanted to be fed by the missionaries. See John 6 verse 26. Are there any similar people today? How would you describe them?

2. Can you think of other incidents in which Andrew was involved (see John 1 and John 12).

3. Was this a miracle of organisation and sharing rather than a miracle of provision and supply? Discuss.

4. How would you classify this miracle?

5. Are there lessons to be learned from the twelve baskets that were left?

6. What was the great physical-to-spiritual link-up here? Can you give any other 'I am' sayings of Jesus?

CHAPTER 13.

JESUS SPOILS A FUNERAL PARTY!   Luke chapter 7 verse 7-17

Soon afterwards, Jesus went to a town called Nain, and His disciples and a large crowd went along with Him.   As He approached the town gate, a dead person was being carried out – the only son of his mother, and she was a widow. And a large crowd from the town was with her. When the Lord saw her, His heart went out to her, and He said, 'Don't cry.'

Then he went up and touched the coffin, and those carrying it stood still. He said, 'Young man, I say to you, get up!' The dead man sat up, and began to talk, and Jesus gave him back to his mother.

They were all filled with awe and praised God. 'A great prophet has appeared among us,' they said. 'God has come to help His people.' The news about Jesus spread throughout Judaea and the surrounding country.

JESUS SPOILS A FUNERAL PARTY.

We have attempted to explain that miracles were acts of wonder, acts of power, or acts of significance, self-authenticating signs which are embedded in the Gospels to reveal that Jesus was and is the Son of God. I also gave a simple division of the miracles as nature miracles and healing miracles. It is hard to classify the narrative concerning the Widow of Nain and her son. It belongs to a stupendous sub-class involving Jesus in raising the dead, which includes the raising of Jairus' daughter, and the raising of Lazarus. Let's get going by listening to Peterson's paraphrase 'The Message', Luke chapter 7 verses 11-17.

'Not long after that, Jesus went to the village Nain. His disciples were with Him, along with quite a large crowd. As they approached the village gate, they met a funeral procession – a woman's only son was being carried out for burial. And the mother was a widow. When Jesus saw her, His heart broke. He said to her, 'Don't cry.' Then he went over and touched the coffin. The pall-bearers stopped. He said : 'Young man, I tell you. Get up.' The dead son sat up and began talking. Jesus presented him to his mother.
They all realised they were in a place of holy mystery, that God was at work among them. They were quietly worshipful – and then noisily grateful, calling out among themselves, 'God is back, looking at the needs of His people!' The news of Jesus spread through the country.'

What an awful time women have had in the world, both ancient and modern! I apologise for my gender, ladies! No wonder feminists have retaliated with sayings like 'when God made Adam, He was just practising', and so on...
Plato said a bad man's fate would be to be reincarnated as a woman. Aristotle regarded a female as a kind of mutilated male. He wrote: 'Females are imperfect males, accidentally produced by the father's inadequacy...' Gandhi wrote in his autobiography 'A Hindu husband regards himself as lord and master of his wife, who must ever dance attendance on him'. Sura 4 of the Koran says 'men have authority over women because Allah has made the one superior to the other ...as for those from whom you fear disobedience, admonish them and send them to beds apart, and beat them.'

Jewish writers, not just Greek philosophers and Hindu and Moslem writers, were equally scathing. Josephus said women were inferior to men in every way. In the Jewish form of morning prayer, a Jewish man had to give thanks that he was not born a Gentile, a slave a woman or a prisoner... The implication was that Eve brought Adam into sin. Some ladies have also thought that this was 'a sigh of relief' prayer, because thereby men were spared the pain of childbirth. In Jewish law a woman was a husband's chattel, with no legal rights. Men could divorce their wives for the most trivial things, like how they looked in the morning, or if they happened to burn the food.

Christian writers were also abusive, despite the plain teaching as far back as the Book of Genesis:

'So God created man in His own image. In the image of God He created him; male and female He created them. God blessed them and said to them, 'Be fruitful and increase in number; fill the earth and subdue it. Rule over the fish of the sea and the birds of the air and over every living creature that moves on the ground.' (Genesis 1 verses 26-28). Human beings therefore have a bond with their Creator, a blessing to unite and multiply, and a duty to dominate creation. Men and women were made equal beneficiaries of the stamp of God and the subduing of earth.

In the Old Testament, women assembled with men and children to hear the Torah read, and the qualities of a good wife were praised in Proverbs 31. Marriage was based on Yahweh's loving relationship to His covenant people. Good women like Hannah, Abigail Ruth and Esther were honoured.
Yet by around AD200 Tertullian, the Early Church Father says: ' You are the devil's gateway; you are the unsealer of that forbidden tree: you are the first deserter of that divine law; you are she who persuaded him whom the devil was not valiant enough to attack. You destroyed so easily God's image, man. On account of you....even the Son of God had to die.'

The status and service of women changed in the 20th century AD for the better. The sterling work done by women in munition factories and public transport, coupled with the agitation of the suffragettes, won the vote after World War I, and they could apply for public office after the Sex Disqualificaton (Removal) Act of 1919. Things have moved very slowly. In 1970 the top managers of American corporate companies were 99% male. By 2005 , 95% of top companies were men. At this rate, it will be the year 2270 before women reach parity. Pornography is an irritating and constant reminder of how women can be degraded. In a fine example of his own purple prose John Stott (an 85 year old bachelor by the way) writes : There is no doubt that in many cultures women have been treated as mere playthings and sex objects, as unpaid cooks, housekeepers and childminders, and as brainless simpletons incapable of engaging in rational discussion. Their gifts have been unappreciated, their personality smothered, their freedom curtailed and their service in some areas exploited, in others refused.' Well spoken, John!

We must also consider Jesus' treatment of women, and this widow in particular, who lived in the town of Nain.

Nain, or Nein as it is known today, is a small town in Galilee, 6 miles south-east of Nazareth, a day's journey from Capernaum. The Gospels give a fair amount of information about Jesus in relation to women. He was 'born of a woman' a 'highly favoured' young woman, some would say a teenager, 'blessed among women', worthy of our honour if not our worship. Mary was not a sinless girl, or her spirit could not have rejoiced in God her Saviour, as she sang in the Magnificat. The status of women was automatically raised in that when Jesus chose to take our flesh, He humbly chose the Virgin's womb.

Jesus submitted to the ethos of the family home set up by Joseph and Mary in Nazareth. In the narrative of the wedding feast in John chapter 2 and from the Cross, Jesus addresses Mary as 'dear lady' and finds time in the heat of His agony to ask the apostle John to treat Mary as Mum. In His public ministry He had a support group of ladies who provided for Him. John chapter 4 tells us how Jesus spends time in theological discussion with a Samaritan woman who had lived an immoral life. It was risky venture because as a Rabbi on His own he was compromised as far as current thought went. She was one of the mongrel group from the North despised by Orthodox Jews. And her lifestyle could have involved Him as the victim of seduction. Jesus treated her questions seriously, and dealt with her gently, refusing to condemn her. Jesus crossed many conventional barriers in His treatment of women. He received a sinful woman in public three times. He allowed a prostitute to come behind Him and drench His feet with her tears, and wipe them with her hair, and cover them with kisses. He accepted her love as an expression of gratitude for her forgiveness. Jesus defended the woman who had been caught in the very act of adultery with great skill and tenderness. (Where was the man who was her partner in adultery?!). He exposed the sin of her accusers without in any way condoning her sin. Jesus allowed Mary of Bethany to sit at His feet and listen to His teaching. This was anathema to regular Jewish tradition, firstly because Mary had assumed the role of a man, and secondly, teaching a woman in this way would be regarded as a waste of time, because of her intellectual inferiority.

It is vital for us to notice that Jesus entrusted the message that He had risen to the ladies who came to the tomb on the first Easter Sunday morning. The touching post-resurrection appearance of Jesus to Mary Magdalene, when she initially mistook Him for the gardener, was very significant evidence of Jesus' regard for women.
So, dear ladies, you can join me in this deep conviction I have that, whereas I have been disappointed sometimes in God's earthly representatives, I have never been disappointed in God's Saviour. If you feel devalued by those around you, or are being ill-treated by the men in your life, remember you are greatly valued by God. Jesus is worthy of your total trust, and will never let you down...

Can you imagine what a study in contrasts these two processions must have presented? Here is one going towards the entrance to the town of Nain, with the Lord of Life, the Lord Jesus Christ as its focus, surrounded by a joyful and expectant crowd. The other was coming out of town heading for the local cemetery, with the Lad of Death and his grieving mother as its focus, united in misery at his loss. The emphasis in this miracle story, recorded only by Luke whose Gospel shows a special interest in women, is on the compassion of the Lord Jesus rather than the faith of the woman. Keith Warrington says: 'The Supreme Saviour takes the initiative – authority and sovereignty are combined in simple command.

The **PLIGHT OF THE LADY** is obvious. First of all, she has **no spouse**, no man to stand by her, no backing to provide for normal funeral hospitality. In the culture of the period a woman without a husband was scarcely a normal person. Secondly, she has **no son,** cut off before his prime, the one on whom all her hopes had been concentrated after the death of her husband. Thirdly, she has **no security.** She is therefore devoid of **protection**, except perhaps for ageing parents, although perhaps they had already died in a culture with short life expectancy. Her home and person would be vulnerable in the absence of a man to defend her. She is also devoid of **provision**. There was no State system of welfare provision, social security, widow's pension – forget all that stuff. Her chances of finding gainful employment would be very low. All she had left were happy memories cut short, snuffed out by death.

No wonder Death is called the Grim Reaper. Her only hope lay in Jesus the Stranger of Galilee, and she possibly had never heard of Him. But He was near. Perhaps I am writing to someone, or several people who have been recently bereaved. The crowds have gone away, the family have returned to their normal duties and the responsibilities of their work and their children, and you feel alone. Listen! The living Lord Jesus Christ is near you, and He can help...We've been highlighting **the Plight of the Lady,** now we must move our centre of gravity to look at the **Power of the Lord**. In fact, this is the first time in his Gospel that Doctor Luke refers to Jesus as 'the Lord'. It's a very suitable title, because here Jesus is the Master of the situation, and He is about to prove He is Lord of the dead as well as the living. The narrative has all the hallmarks of an eye-witness account.

We see the Power of the Lord in **the Pity He Showed.** First of all there is the look of Jesus. He saw the desperate need of the woman. Dr Campbell Morgan wrote: 'Jesus always has eyes for the brokenhearted.' He took in the situation at a glance. Then there is the **Presence He Shared.** He went over to the widow, who would have been walking in front of the cortege, and told her to dry her tears, and stop crying. He then approached the bier. The word 'coffin' in Peterson's translation is a bit misleading. It is probable that the dead youth's body was wrapped in a shroud, and placed on a movable frame. Then Jesus touched the frame on which the lad's body was placed. This was a quiet signal for the bearers to stop, and halt the procession. Incidentally, such contact near a dead body meant that Jesus was defiled according to ceremonial law. In meeting human need, Jesus deliberately ignored ceremonial rules and regulations. Pity stood above Pollution in His agenda. Thirdly, we see the Power of the Lord in the **Pronouncement He Made.** He spoke to the young man. Here Jesus' power was operating in an area beyond our ken, in a way which marked Him out as the Son of God. Here He underlines the verdict pronounced on Him elsewhere – 'Nobody ever spoke like this man.'

There is a qualitative distinction here between Jesus and any other prophet or religious leader since. The young man sat up, began to speak, and, with a beautiful finale to this great drama, Jesus gave him back to his mother. In the three resurrection stories in the Gospels, Jesus spoke to the dead person – to the lovely twelve year old daughter of Jairus, and Jesus' friend, Lazarus- and He does so here. Jesus speaks with the voice that wakens the dead! He also rules over the spirit world beyond our ken..Some scholars say the lad was in a cataleptic trance, and the miracle here was that Jesus prevented him from being buried alive. There is no evidence to back this up in the narrative. Luke faithfully records the awe-stricken crowd.

No wonder Jesus said later: 'All authority in heaven and on earth has been given to me.' What do you think of Jesus today? Was he sad or bad or mad or God? For millions of Christians around the world, including your author, He is the Son of God, worthy of anyone's deepest trust...

We'll round things off by looking at **The Praise of the Crowd.** We can look at this in two ways: First of all, their **WONDER**. Peterson's translation says: 'they all realised that they were in a place of holy mystery, that God was at work among them. They were quietly worshipful...' They were technically correct, but inadequate in their grasp of the divine nature of Jesus. They said 'a great prophet has appeared among us'(Luke 7 verse 16)...They also said 'God has come to help His people'. The One before them, Jesus of Nazareth, the Man of Galilee, was also God Incarnate.

In just seven verses of the Bible, we are introduced to Jesus the Miracle-Maker, mega-style, as our American brethren would say. And what He did in the physical realm, He can replicate in the spiritual realm, raising us from our moribund state to a state of being alive in Christ. Charles Studd, a former England cricketer with a straight bat and a big balance which he gave away to Christian work, said 'If Jesus Christ be God, and died for me, then no sacrifice is too great for me to make for Him.'

QUESTIONS.

1. What circumstances gave the widow a bleak outlook?

2. See Acts chapter 6 verse 1, and James 1 verse 27. Has the Welfare State done away with the church's special responsibilities for orphans and widows? Discuss.

3. How does Luke stress the state of the lady from Nain? In what ways does Jesus identify with the grief described here?

4. Does our culture have any special customs and beliefs about death? What are they, and how should Christians react to them?

5. What is the Biblical view of the role of women, and wives?

6. Discuss your ideas about the role of women in the church.

CHAPTER 14

THE DEAF MAN FROM DECAPOLIS
Mark Chapter 7 verses 31-37.

Then Jesus left the vicinity of Tyre and went through Sidon, down to the Sea of Galilee and into the region of the Decapolis.

There some people brought to Him a man who was deaf and could hardly talk, and they begged Him to place His hand on the man.

After He took him aside, away from the crowd, Jesus put His fingers into the man's ears. Then He spit and touched the man's tongue. He looked up to heaven and with a deep sigh said to him, 'Ephphatha!' (which means 'be opened'). At this, the man's ears were opened, his tongue was loosened, and he began to speak plainly.

Jesus commanded them not to tell anyone. But the more He did so, the more they kept talking about it. People were overwhelmed with amazement. 'He has done everything well,' they said. 'He even makes the deaf hear and the mute speak.'

THE DEAF MAN FROM DECAPOLIS

If you want to keep it simple, and who doesn't? , the message of the Bible can be summarised in three phrases :   The King will Come (Old Testament).....The King has Come (Gospels, Acts and New Testament Letters)....The King will Come Again (The Book of Revelation and a recurring theme throughout the New Testament).   The message of God's Gospel, or Good News can also be summed up in three phrases ; God is.... (ie He exists) God is Love... God Loves Me. In the narrative we are looking at today, Jesus demonstrates the love of God in a healing miracle, or self-authenticating sign, in dealing with a deaf mute from the Decapolis (The Ten Towns), an area South of the Sea of Galilee, and East of the River Jordan. These ten towns had formed a trading league since about AD1. Here is Peterson's version of the story from Mark chapter 8 verses 31 to 35:

'Then Jesus left the region of Tyre, went through Sidon back to Galilee Lake, and over to the district of the Ten Towns. Some people brought a man who could neither hear nor speak and asked Jesus to lay a healing hand on him. He took the man off by himself, put His fingers in the man's ears and some spit on the man's tongue. Then Jesus looked up in prayer, groaned mightily, and commanded , 'Ephphatha – Open Up!' And it happened. The man's hearing was clear and his speech plain – just like that.

Jesus urged them to keep quiet, but they talked it up all the more, beside themselves with excitement.   'He's done it all, and done it well. He gives hearing to the deaf, speech to the speechless.'

Perhaps you would like to hear the story in broad Scots. Professor Lorimer was an expert in Scots and Greek – he was Professor of Greek at St Andrews University, and his translation is very accurate. Are you sitting quietly? The word processor may explode, but here goes:

'Efter that Jesus quat the kintra o Tyre again an fuir bi Sidon owre tae the Loch o Galilee an intil the mids o the Ten touns' kintra. There they brocht til Him a tung-tackit deifie and socht Him tae lay His haund on him. Jesus tuik the man awa frae the croud his lane an stappit his fingers intil his lugs an pat a lick o His spittin on his tung, an syne, luikin up intil the lift, said til him wi an unco sech 'Ephphatha', whilk is the Aramaic for 'Be apent'. Wi that the man's lugs wis apent, an the tack o his tung was swackent, and he begoud speakin the same as ither fowk. Jesus baud them say nocht o the matter til onie-ane: but the mair He baud them, the mair eydentlie they trokit the news aa-wey an athort, an aabody wis ondeemouslie dumfoonert: 'Braw an bonnie wark, aa this o His,' said they, 'garrin een the deif hear an the dumb speak!'

The miracle story in this chapter is an illustration of how Jesus showed compassion. The New Testament Gospels, which was written in Greek originally, tell us explicitly 12 times that Jesus was moved with compassion. Although the term was not used here, the concept is certainly present here in the actions of Jesus. The Greek verb is 'splanchnizomai' which means 'to be moved with compassion', which means 'to be viscerally affected', or 'to have a gut reaction' to human need. The splanchna are what William Barclay calls 'the nobler viscera, namely the heart liver, lungs, and intestines, which were regarded as the seat of the human emotions.' When Jesus saw this poor man, His heart went out to him. In the Gospels, every time Jesus was moved with compassion, He always did something to meet the need of the people in front of Him – He fed the crowd, he taught them, He touched the leper, and so on.

One of the Early Church writers, Eusebius, who wrote his 'Ecclesiastical History' around AD 300, wrote about Jesus: He was like some excellent physician, who, in order to cure the sick, examines what is repulsive, handles sores and reaps pain himself from the sufferings of others.' William Barclay says 'Jesus regarded the sufferer and the needy with a pity which issued in help.'

When you think about it, sometimes we say 'that was a moving experience,' but we should ask ourselves 'where was I moved to? What was I moved to DO as a result of this moving experience?' The emotion Jesus felt obviously moved Him to the depths of His being, and stirred Him into action. Here Jesus was touched by the man with a double difficulty. Often people with hearing difficulties have also speech problems. The problem of deafness has not gone away. There are just under 9 million deaf and hard of hearing people in the UK, and about 2 million of us have hearing aids. 2.3 million have tinnitus. Scotland has about 750,000 people with moderate or severe deafness. People who also have speech difficulties don't like to be called 'deaf and dumb' or 'deaf and mute'. I remember once totally misjudging one of my students who sat near the front of the lecture hall. She turned out to be one of my brightest students, and I had misjudged her on her appearance. She was intent on hearing what I said, and I had to ask for the Lord's forgiveness for a wrong attitude to this lass. Jesus was a perfect person who was totally sensitive to the need around Him, and moved quickly to help the man in the narrative.

The Christian message highlights the perfection of Christ's character. On the first Christmas, he came to earth as the baby of a peasant girl, who married his foster-father Joseph the carpenter of Nazareth. When a child was born, thank-offerings were made to God according to the means at the disposal of the parents. At Jesus' birth, Mary and Joseph made the offering that poor people brought, two turtle-doves or two young pigeons. Jesus was part of a big family – he had four brothers and at least two sisters, and in His later teaching He refers to patched clothes, and one-roomed houses. He knew about ordinary life in a small town.

The New Testament argues strongly about His real humanity – he faced temptation without falling to it. HR MackIntosh argued that because His humanity was not damaged or blunted by sin, for Jesus temptation must have been the most exquisite torture. The perfection of His nature would have made Him extraordinarily sensitive to those around Him – like the deaf man in this miracle. The first component for a work of God in this incident was **THE LOOK OF COMMUNION**. The text says in verse 34 'He looked up to heaven'. My blessed Lord Jesus lived in constant communion with His Father God, so there was no real need for Him to do this. He looked up to heaven here to remind the crowd of His intimate contact with God the Father. Something spectacularly worthwhile was about to happen, and it happened because Jesus lived in daily and constant communion with God. When you or I put our hand in the hand of the Man who stilled the water, we are in touch with heavenly realities. And if we want to be used by God to do some work for Him, we have to sense His presence, and live in communion with Him. There was a young Presbyterian minister in Dundee called Robert Murray McCheyne. He died when he was 29, but he saw a tremendous spiritual awakening among his congregation before he died. He said 'my people's greatest need is my personal holiness.'

The second component for a work of God, here the work of Jesus healing a profoundly deaf man with speech difficulties, is **THE SIGH OF COMPASSION**. Verse 34 here refers to a deep sigh, what Lorimer's translation calls 'an unco sech'. We have noted the meaning of compassion already.

Human misery profoundly affected the Lord Jesus Christ. It must have provided the greatest possible contrast to the constant joy of heaven. Three times in the New Testament it tells us that Jesus wept. When He surveyed Jerusalem on His last journey there, He wept over the city, for He longed to gather its people like a hen gathers her chickens to her for security, warmth and protection. When His friend Lazarus of Bethany died, He wept over the family. He loves families. And before He went through the agonies of Gethsemane and Calvary, he wept over a tyranny – the tyranny of sin and death whose power He came to break. The plight of lost and helpless people made Him groan. He felt so sorry for this man. Where are our tears for the generation in which we live? I watched an item on television news recently about joy-riders damaging themselves and killing others, including a lovely five year old boy. Recently, I conducted the cremation service of a young woman who had been sleeping rough in Glasgow. She drunk herself to death. In her earlier life she had a baby boy, and her boyfriend took the baby and gave him to her parents to bring up. The elderly man who took her off the street was unable to help her break her habits, and the saddest thing was when the funeral party filed into the crematorium, there were six people at her funeral, apart from the undertaker and myself. The sadness of this man's plight broke Jesus' heart, and He sighed with compassion. Our macho man culture says men don't cry, but I cried last week, and felt a certain affinity with Jesus. Could we do anything to help? What about showing compassion to someone this Christmas? Please forgive me if I have upset you with these sad realities.

We are looking at the narrative from Mark's Gospel chapter 7 verses 31-37. Jesus healed a deaf man with a speech impediment, and we're thinking about the four essentials for a work of God from this story. So far, we've seen the **LOOK of COMMUNION**, and the **SIGH of COMPASSION**. The third one is **THE TOUCH OF CONTACT**. Sometimes we complain about people who are 'too touchy-feely', but when you consider the man in this story, we can understand Jesus' actions here. Being deaf and unable to speak must be very alienating, and isolating. Jesus took him away from the crowd, aside on his own, so that he could concentrate and understand Jesus' personal interest in him. He was not a case, he was a person, to Jesus. Then he put His fingers into the man's ears, the focal point of his troubles, and Jesus spat and touched his tongue. The ancient world believed in the curative power of saliva. The various gestures of Jesus were meant to show the deaf man by sign language what Jesus intended to do. Jesus applied His power to the man's situation in a visual, tactile way. The whole story has the hallmark of an eyewitness account.

There is a big difference between the negative holiness of separation and the positive holiness of dedication and application. Some people think the quietness of the monastery or the cloister is the only way to practice holiness. The great Protestant reformer Martin Luther went into an Augustinian monastery in 1505. As a Roman Catholic monk and priest he was interested only in reforming himself, and engaged in a fierce search for holiness. He took death, judgement, heaven and eternal fire very seriously, and was tormented and terrified at his first saying of Mass. He said 'I am dust and ashes and full of sin, and I am speaking to the living, the eternal, and the true God.' He prayed and fasted, went to confession and wore out his confessor at six-hour-long sessions, went on pilgrimage to Rome and crawled up the Scala Sancta saying Hail Marys on every step, searching for holiness. He eventually found peace, as he put it 'Sola fides, sola gratia, sola Scriptura' = 'By faith alone, by grace alone, by Scripture alone.' The positive holiness of dedication and application is seen here as Jesus is in the thick of things in a crowd, dealing specifically with an individual in need.

In the late nineteenth and early twentieth century, there was a famous preacher in Manchester, a Scot called Alexander Maclaren. He was a very skilful expositor, and his commentary on the letter to the Colossians in the Exposiror's Bible series has never been bettered. The Manchester Guardian used to print his Sunday morning sermon in full in its Monday issue. I have altered and up-dated his words, but here's one of the things he said. 'You'll never clean up the street by standing at the end of it with an aerosol can, saying 'Be thou clean'. If you want to clean up the street, you've got to get involved with the filth. Jesus got involved with the filth.' The TOUCH OF CONTACT is necessary...

We must be careful as we study how Jesus healed a man who could neither hear or speak, who had existed for years in that silent world, unable to hear or talk.
We have linked to this story the four criteria which are components of a work of God. The first three were : **THE LOOK OF COMMUNION, THE SIGH OF COMPASSION, AND THE TOUCH OF CONTACT**. The fourth one is **THE WORD OF COMMAND**. Jesus spoke to the man in his own language, Aramaic. The word of command was 'Ephphatha'. Imagine! The first word the man heard were in the local dialect. It was like speaking Gaelic to a true Highlander. The word is one of the Aramaic fragments preserve in the New Testament, like Abba (dear daddy), Talitha cumi (wee lassie, get up), eloi eloi lama sabachtani (my God, my God, why have you forsaken me), and Marana tha (please Lord, come). The word 'ephphatha' means 'be opened' but it could possibly also mean 'be delivered, or released' (the Old Testament equivalent is used of setting camels free, or opening a crocodile's jaws).

One of the things which really upset the Jewish leaders who were Jesus' opponents was that He spoke with authority. This was a word of command from Jesus the Healer. In Matthew 28 verse 19 Jesus claimed that all authority (the Greek word 'exousia' means rightful authority from a legitimate source) in heaven and earth was given to Him. The deaf man's hearing was set free to function, and he would no longer be 'tongue-tied', but set free to relate to the world in which he lived, to speak plainly. Jesus had dealt with him privately and sensitively, and Jesus told the man to keep it quiet, probably out of consideration for what new-found celebrity would do to him. With typical perversity, the more he warned them, the more they talked! Their verdict is nevertheless a good and sound one 'He has done everything well!' He even makes the deaf hear and the dumb speak'. There's a hymn in the old edition of the Baptist Hymn Book (it's a sign of becoming an old grump when you moan about them missing out your favourite hymns), which says:

Lord, I was blind, I could not see in Thy marred visage any grace....
Lord I was deaf, I could not hear the thrilling music of Thy voice...
Lord, I was dumb, I could not speak the grace and glory of Thy Name...
Lord, I was dead, I could not stir my lifeless soul to come to Thee...
 That all changed for the man in the story, and it can change spiritually for you and me....

QUESTIONS.

1. How did the crowd show its excitement about Jesus' healing powers?

2. Are deafness and speech problems related complaints?

3. How did Jesus help the situation so that the man could concentrae and have Jesus' attention?

4. Specify in detail what visual and tactile signals Jesus gave to help the deaf man.   Should Christians be careful/restrained/outgoing in their body language?

5. What verbal sign of personal interest did Jesus show? How would that help the man's condition?

6. What were the pitfalls of popularity for Jesus here?

7. What are the pitfalls of popularity for a modern servant of God?

CHAPTER 15
THE MADMAN AND THE PIGS   Luke chapter 8 verses 26-39

They sailed to the region of the Gerasenes, which is across the lake from Galilee.

When Jesus stepped ashore, He was met by a demon-possessed man from the tombs. For a long time his man had not worn clothes or lived in a house, but had lived in the tombs.

When he saw Jesus, he cried out and fell at His feet, shouting at the top of his voice, 'What do you want with me, Jesus, Son of the Most High God? I beg you, don't torture me!' For Jesus had commanded the evil spirit to come out of the man. Many times it had seized him, and though he was chained hand and foot and kept under guard, he had broken his chains and had been driven by the demon into solitary places.

Jesus asked him 'What is your name?'   'Legion,' he replied, because many demons had gone into him. And they begged Him repeatedly not to order them to go into the Abyss.

A large herd of pigs was feeding there on the hillside. The demons begged Jesus to let them go into them, and He gave them permission. When the demons came out of the man, they went into the pigs and the herd rushed down the steep bank into the lake and was drowned.

When those tending the pigs saw what had happened, they ran off and reported this in the town and countryside, and the people went out to see what had happened. When they came to Jesus, they found the man from whom the demons had gone out, sitting at Jesus' feet, dressed and in his right mind; and they were afraid. Those who had seen it told how the demon-possessed man had been cured. Then all the people of the region of the Gerasenes asked Jesus to leave them, because they were overcome with fear. So he got into the boat and left.

The man from whom the demons gone out begged to go with Him, but Jesus sent him away, saying, 'Return home and tell how much God has done for you.' So the man went away and told all over the town how much Jesus had done for him.

THE MADMAN AND THE PIGS.

We are looking at some of the miracle stories from the Gospels. We started off looking at some definition of a miracle, which is more than something unusual, like Partick Thistle or even Clyde, beating Celtic. A miracle is way off the normal. It seems to defy the laws of nature or science, and even where there is a naturalistic explanation, it is the timing that retains the miraculous element. Today's miracle brings Jesus into the arena of demon possession, for Legion, the wild man of the tombs, was a tortured soul tormented by demonic powers. It is the most extensive exorcism narrative in the New Testament. This is all fascinating stuff for today's society. Before we dive into it, here is Doctor Luke's account in 'The Message' translation:

'They sailed on to the country of the Gerasenes, directly opposite Galilee. As He stepped out onto land, a madman from town met Him; he was a victim of demons. He hadn't worn clothes for a long time, nor lived at home; he lived in the cemetery. When he saw Jesus, He screamed, fell before Him, and bellowed, 'What business do you have messing with me? You're Jesus, Son of the High God, but don't give me a hard time! (the man said this because Jesus had started to order the unclean spirit out of him.)

Time after time the demon threw the man into convulsions. He had been placed under constant guard and tied with chains and shackles, but crazed and driven wild by the demon, he would shatter the bonds.
Jesus asked him, 'What is your name?'
'Mob. My name is Mob,' he said, because many demons afflicted him. And they begged Jesus desperately not to order them to the bottomless pit.

A large herd of pigs was browsing and rooting on a nearby hill. The demons begged Jesus to order them into the pigs. He gave the order. It was even worse for the pigs. Crazed, they stampeded over a cliff into the lake and drowned.
Those tending the pigs, scared to death, bolted and told their story in town and country. People went out to see what had happened. They came to Jesus and found the man from whom the demons had been sent, sitting there at Jesus' feet wearing decent clothes and making sense. It was a holy moment, and for a short time they were more reverent than curious. Then those who had seen it happen told how the demoniac had been saved.

Later, a great many people from Gerasene countryside got together and asked Jesus to leave - too much change, too fast, and they were scared. So Jesus got back in the boat and set off. The man whom He had delivered from the demons asked to go with Him, but He sent him back, saying, 'Go home and tell everything God did in you.' So he went back and preached all over town everything Jesus had done in him.' Jesus had just stilled a fierce storm, and brought a great calm. Now He would bring lasting peace into the heart and life of a demoniac.

Our view of the New Testament picture of this tormented soul will vary according to our attitude to the Bible. Many folk have no problem with this sort of description. They regard it as part of the mythology of the New

Testament, something not to be taken literally. They would say that this is merely evidence of primitive superstitious belief in demons, which could nowadays could be explained in terms of mental illness. They would say that belief in Satan and the Devil is in a similar category, part of the 'wrapping-paper' which modern people have to strip off in order to get to the principles behind the text.

'Men don't believe in a devil now as their fathers used to do
They've forced the door of the broadest creed to let his majesty through
There isn't a print of his cloven hoof, or a fiery dart from his bow
To be seen in the earth or the air today, for the world has voted so...
Of course the Devil's ceased to be, of course the Devil's gone,
But simple people want to know – who carries his business on ?!

There is a tremendous interest in the supernatural, and especially what people call 'the darker side' in today's world. Films like 'The Exorcist' 'Rosemary's Baby', 'Poltergeist' and the 'Omen' series have spawned a huge crop of others in this specialist genre. Every station bookshop has magazines on Tarot, Fortune-telling, Witchcraft, Ouija, the Occult, and Britain now has a Church of Satan, and Joy of Satan ministries openly declares 'There is no god but myself...knowing this, who dares worship the false gods of the Koran and the Bible.' A local librarian told me the shelves on the occult are the busiest in the library. Young people are sporting tattoos and t-shirts with demonic slogans and designs. Our television programmes regularly include interviews with witches. Many people who reject church are quite willing to say that they are 'spiritual people' with what they would say was a broad-minded, open-ended approach to the supernatural.

Within the Christian church there is a group of believers with specialist interests in these things. Some seem to have a perception of demonic activity on a widespread scale, and are involved in exorcism of demons from people and homes as part of a Christian healing ministry. A few were influenced by a book entitled 'Pigs in the Parlour' whose author lived in a world infested by demons. I have to admit that I have been involved in exorcism, but only on the fringe of my Christian ministry. Some of my missionary friends who work in different cultures overseas express heightened awareness of occult activity and demon possession there. It would be helpful to compare and contrast possession and mental illness.

Sometimes the story under consideration is named 'The Healing of Legion', or 'Mob' as he is sometimes called. There are aspects of the madman's behaviour which exhibit symptoms similar to mental illness - shouting, chaotic behaviour, supernatural strength, indifference to pain, and self-mutilation. Like the madman here, mentally ill patients can be socially rootless and marginalised, and can engage in physical display. About 10% of admissions to modern medical wards in hospitals are due to self-harming. It is a modern phenomenon which is alarming, because it points to unhappy underlying symptoms like stress, anger, aggression, and frustration. It is inadequate simply to categorise it as attention-seeking behaviour. People cut their arms, legs, face, abdomen, breasts and even their genitals. They inflict blows on themselves, bang against things, and insert sharp objects under their skin or into their bodily orifices.

Despite the similarities, there is a qualitative difference between possession and mental illness, and discernment is required. There are scary bits that take us beyond mere mental illness here. Imagine meeting a violent and dishevelled maniac rushing at you from the tombs, yelling at the top of his voice! We have to admire Jesus' personal courage here.

This miracle is an object lesson on some of Jesus' techniques used in His constant conflict with evil spirits, who were engaged in an unusual eruption of opposition to the work of Jesus. There are only four exorcism stories in the Gospels. Jesus uses confrontation and verbal exchange here. He also uses set formulae like 'Be quiet or be muzzled', 'come out ', and here Jesus asks for the demons' name. The answer 'Mob' or 'Legion' indicates a multi-form possession by a demon regiment (A Roman legion contained 6000 soldiers). Jesus was also able to transfer demons, here from the man to the pigs. Jesus never used apparatus or medicine in His healings. Some scholars have suggested that Mob, or Legion, became unhinged and possessed after witnessing the killing machine, which was the Roman Army, at work – George Adam Smith found the graves of some of the X Legion in Gadara, on the Eastern shore of Galilee.

Bertrand Russell in his book 'Why I am not a Christian' takes exception to what he calls Jesus' cruelty to animals here – the evil spirits go into the pigs, and they are drowned. The maniac would need some verbal demonstration of his deliverance. Another point is that the incident illustrates the relative value of a human life against a large number of pigs. Some have pointed out that if the pigs were owned by Jews, they were probably breaking Jewish food laws and this was apt retribution!

Charles Wesley wrote 'Jesus the Name high over all, in hell or earth or sky, angels and men before it fall, and devils fear and fly.'.....
 I have to confess an affinity with this fascinating narrative. I also have to admit to personal affinities with the story because of my upbringing.

First of all, I have an interest in cemeteries! I was brought up in the Lambhill district of Glasgow, an area which is known as the 'Dead Centre' of Glasgow, because it boasts a Protestant cemetery, a Catholic cemetery, a Jewish cemetery, and in case you thought you'd escaped, a Crematorium!

Secondly, I have to admit a lifelong fascination with pigs! When I was three years old, we moved from Mansion Street in Possilpark to Lochside Cottage, along the canal bank at Lambhill. We had been living with my granny in Possil, and now we had free occupation of the cottage from my dad's pal, who owned Graham's piggery, if my dad would feed his pigs every weekend!

As a wee boy, I was fitted out with dungarees, given a wheelbarrow made by my dad, and allowed to carry charcoal in barrowloads for the boiler, and taught to clean out pigsties. I was given runts from litters of pigs, and my Dad told me to put them in a shoe-box in the oven till they heated up, then I fed them milk from a child's feeding bottle until they were strong enough to return to the litter. I have always found pigs to be clever and lovable creatures!

So now can you understand how a story from the Gospels featuring a cemetery and pigs would interest me?! Thirdly, like the madman in the story, I have experienced the kindness of Christ, who brought me into an experience of a heart at peace and a mind at ease. The narrative recorded here indicates our human predicament, and Christ's divine power. First of all,

Legion found himself in a place of death, but Jesus gave him life.

He ran bellowing at Jesus from the tombs, and finished up sitting, clothed and sensible. Ephesians 2 verse 1 following says, 'As for you, you were dead in your transgressions and sins, in which you used to live when you followed the ways of this world and of the ruler of the kingdom of the air, the spirit who is now at work in those who are disobedient. Back in the Garden of Eden God warned Adam and Eve that disobedience would bring death, and so it did – spiritual death immediately, physical death eventually.

All around us are people who think they are alive, but they are really dead, spiritually, and nothing less than a new birth will bring them into vital living contact with God. My father used to say about one of our relatives who was always complaining about her illnesses, 'She's dead if she had the sense to stiffen'. The madman in the tombs found new life through Jesus' intervention. The apostle Paul describes the common experience of Christian people changed by Jesus : 'If any man is in Christ, he is a new creation; the old has gone, the new has come'.(2 Corinthians 5 v 17). In Ephesians 2 Paul writes ; 'God, who is rich in mercy, made us alive with Christ even when we were dead in transgressions – it is by grace you have been saved.' Perhaps today some of you reading this will come crying to Jesus, and find yourself alive in Him...

Jesus went about doing good and healing those who were oppressed by the devil, like the madman legion, or Mob, in the narrative we are considering.

The first feature in this story, which illustrates the human predicament, and Jesus' divine power, was this:

The Man found himself in a place of Death, and Jesus gave him life.

The second feature is:

The Man found himself in a state of Domination, and Jesus gave him Freedom

Legion was under strong control. His voice, his physical movements, his mental attitude, his isolated surroundings all speak of domination. His was a multi-form possession by a veritable regiment of demons, and his wounds were self-inflicted. He really presents a striking picture of today's society – in a state of domination. They tell us that obesity, and especially teenage obesity, is an emerging threat in Britain. I remember years ago that Orson Welles the actor said America had become 'pudding-faced.' Who was he to talk? - but the fact is fat people are dominated by thoughts of food. They cannot rationalise their obesity by saying they have big bones or a thick skin. Some say that inside every fat person is a thin person trying to get out. The truth is the opposite. Outside every fat person there is a fatter person trying to get in.

Similarly, our biggest narcotic drug, alcohol, holds many in the grip of its domination. Food and booze are killers, and on the way we are contracting diabetes at unprecedented levels. Brits are also dominated by gambling, especially the lottery and the card game poker. People opposed to the building of a super casino in Glasgow pointed out that it would result in a huge increase of gambling addicts. Some harmful drugs, we are told, are becoming as cheap as sweeties, but the bondage they bring is super-serious.

I recently visited Barlinnie Prison, Glasgow, and was told that a large percentage of our huge prison population are 'recidivist prisoners' or repeat offenders who keep committing the same crimes. The worst thing about our human predicament is that, apart from Christ's intervention and grace, we are all recidivist sinners, needing His deliverance. Jesus set this man free, and He can set us free. He can deliver us from any dominating evil influences, and give us real freedom. Jesus said 'If the Son (referring to Himself) shall set you free, you will be free indeed.' Just like there are people all around us who think they are alive and they are really dead, so there are people all around us who think they are free, and they are really prisoners. Jesus is our only hope. Charles Wesley wrote;

> 'Long my imprisoned spirit lay fast bound in sin and nature's night, Thine eye diffused a quickening ray, I woke, the dungeon flamed with light. My chains fell off, my heart was free, I rose, went forth and followed Thee.'

Jesus was, and is, a Miracle-Maker. The maniac from the tombs wanted to go with Him, but Jesus sent him back to his home area to be a powerful witness to the grace and power of the Lord Jesus Christ. You could make a huge difference if you turned to Him for new Life and Freedom and Hope.

This is the third feature of Legion as he appears in this miracle story. **Remember: 1. He was in a place of death and Jesus gave him life. 2. He was in a state of domination, and Jesus gave him Freedom. Thirdly, he was in a situation of despair, and Jesus gave him Hope.** He was lonely, scared and desperate before Jesus came. He was isolated from society. His connection with the cemetery probably meant he was considered ritually unclean therefore not allowed to worship at Temple or synagogue. He came and pleaded for Jesus to show him mercy. Even the demons which controlled him recognised that Jesus was 'The Son of the Most high God'. He was in despair, in the clutches of strong forces, robbed of hope. Do you know any people like that? Sometimes we deliberately avoid people whose despair seems to be contagious. Yet Jesus gave this man a double hope, which became a reality in his life.

Firstly, there was the hope of transformation, realised when the neighbours saw the man from whom the demons had gone out sitting, clothed and in his right mind.   Secondly, there was the hope of testimony, probably evident in his behaviour and his shining face, and in his obedience to do what Jesus told him : 'Return home, and tell how much God has done for you.'   A good occupation for an ex-maniac, don't you think?

QUESTIONS.

1. How can we distinguish between mental illness and demon possession? Is a depressive state a special category?

2. Is demon possession present in today's society? How can we recognise and respond to it?

3. How did Legion's state reflect his relation to the people of the Ten Towns? (=Decapolis)

4. How did the demons react to Jesus? What evidence showed it was multi possession here?

5 Why would Legion want the demons to go into the pigs? Was this cruelty to animals? Discuss.

6. What evidences of exit of the demons and change in Legion were there?

7. do modern Christians have power to cast out demons? Share.

CHAPTER 16.

THE MIRACLE OF CHRISTMAS Matthew Chapter 1 verses 18-25.

This is how the birth of Jesus Christ came about: His mother Mary was pledged to be married to Joseph, but before they came together, she was found to be with child through the Holy Spirit. Because Joseph her husband was a righteous man and did not want to expose her to public disgrace, he had in mind to divorce her quietly.

But after he had considered this, an angel of the Lord appeared to him in a dream and said, 'Joseph son of David, do not be afraid to take Mary home as your wife, because what is conceived in her is from the Holy Spirit. She will give birth to a son, and you are to give Him the name Jesus, because He will save His people from their sins.'

All this took place to fulfil what the Lord had said through the prophet: 'The virgin will be with child and will give birth to a son, and they will call Him 'Immanuel' – which means 'God with us.'

When Joseph woke up, he did what the angel of the lord had commanded him and took Mary home as his wife. But he had no union with her until she gave birth to a son. And he gave Him the name Jesus.

THE MIRACLE OF CHRISTMAS.

In this chapter, we are standing off-subject a little to look at the miracle of Christmas, when Jesus was born, which ranks second only to the Resurrection of Jesus in the Miracle Stakes. Let me give a cluster of illustrations which might make things clearer.

When Humbert, the great French naturalist, was a boy, he was out walking with his dad. He saw a group of ants scurrying across the dirt path in front of them. 'Dad', he said, 'How can I let the ants know that I don't mean them any harm? ' 'I don't see how you could do that, son, unless you became an ant yourself!' In a way this is what Christmas is all about. God has shown His intentions of love towards us by becoming one of us in the Person of Jesus. This is the Miracle of the Incarnation, the becoming flesh of God. Jesus has given God a face, so to speak.

A few years ago, churches were required by government legislation to provide access for the disabled. In a way, this also illustrates what God has done at the first Christmas. The birth of Jesus, and the whole of what the theologians call 'The Christ-event' - Jesus' birth, life, death and resurrection- has made access to God for people like you and me, who would otherwise be disabled and disqualified from approaching Him.

A town in England put up their Christmas lights, and somebody commented that a bulb had blown. Instead of reading 'Glory to God in the highest', the message from the lights said 'Glory to God in the High Street', so they decided to leave it. The Christmas message is that God has come down to reveal His glory in the High Street as well as the Highest!

One of the great Christians in the Early Church was Augustine who came from Hippo in North Africa. He lived the kind of life that made nice ladies blush, and then he became a Christian, and a top theologian. He described the Christmas message as an important part of paying a debt. He wrote: 'Only man owed the debt, only God could pay the debt. Therefore for God to pay the debt of our sins, God had to become a man...'

To summarise, the miracle of Christmas is that God has come among us. He has come to provide access to God for disabled sinners. He has come to reveal God's glory shining out into our streets, and He has come to pay the debt of our sins. As the Afro-American said, 'I sure done slobbered a bib-full' there.

We are considering the stupendous miracle of Christ's Birth on the first Christmas. We of course hope and pray that you will have a wonderful Christmas every year, that if you have family, you may get together, and if not, you will team up with friends, or be booked in at some hotel. Above all, we hope that you will know the presence and blessing of God wherever you are, and experience the true joy of Christ: 'Joy to the world, the Lord has come!'...

When we come to consider the Virgin Birth, we must put down a few markers before considering alternatives. A large part of the human race believes that the Bible version is to be taken as it stands. Secondly, the birth narratives in

Matthew and Luke (only two out of four Gospels have detailed accounts) do not lend themselves to non-miraculous, non-supernatural explanations. Thirdly, the picture of Jesus elsewhere in the New Testament means to convey that Jesus is the divine Son of God, and is also a perfect human being. Professor William Barclay's definition of Jesus the Messiah takes some beating – 'Never more than a man, never less than God'.

The non-Jewish world would be mystified by the term 'Messiah', who in Old Testament thought was the Anointed One, God's chosen Deliverer. For the Jews at the time of Jesus, there were three distinct views. Firstly, He would be a Breadwinning Provider, for the nation, crippled with tax demands, was poor and hungry. Secondly, He would be a Military General, who would get rid of the Romans, the occupying power at that time. Thirdly, he would be a Holy Superman, an apocalyptic hero coming on the clouds to whisk them away to His heavenly kingdom. These three views are represented in the temptation narratives in the Gospels.

Philo of Alexandria lived around the period of Jesus. He tried to show the close link between Jewish and Greek culture. He claimed that God kept in touch with the world through LOGOS, His word or reason, but he never used the term LOGOS as if it were a person. John took over and went beyond Philo. John saw Jesus as the complete fulfilment of what Philo was searching for. John's Gospel says Jesus was pre-existent and divine, the perfect link between God and men. When John said that the Logos or Word became flesh, he was saying what Philo would never have said. John knew that no sense could be made of the life of Jesus if He was treated by ordinary human standards. Neither the world at large or the Jewish people welcomed Jesus. John was not relating a success story. He was presenting a Messiah who challenged men to believe in Him. The rejection and the challenge are still the same today. What a strange way to begin a Gospel! It begins with a towering concept of Jesus whose glory is that of God's one and only Son, full of all grace and truth. He is still our greatest need in a world full of posers, power-brokers, hooks, crooks and comic singers...

Let us now consider some alternatives to the Christmas story as we have it in the Gospels. We are looking at Jesus the Miracle-maker, and the events of Christmas, one of the greatest miracles in connection with Jesus, and the Virgin Birth. Those rationalists who reject the possibility of miracles and therefore reject the very idea of Virgin Birth, simply reject the Birth stories as unhistorical.

Others see the birth narratives in the Gospels as myth rather than history, religious ideas wrapped up in a historical narrative. The narratives evolved from Old Testament belief that Messiah would be born of a virgin. Some would concede that the genealogies given in Matthew and Luke could have a historical framework.

Other folk think that we have here a Christian adaptation of Jewish or pagan traditions of unusual birth – Isaac, Samuel, Samson, Krishna, and Buddhist traditions, Assyrian/Babylonian, or Zoroastrian sources. Sometimes these births were to elderly or previously infertile couples. Although these are extraordinary births, there are no exact parallels, for example, Siddhartha Gautama the Buddha's mother conceived when a tiny white elephant entered her womb, and Siddhartha was born from her right side without causing her the least pain.

Others say that the present form of the Christmas story in the Gospels are due to editorial activity with the aim of proving that Messiah was the Son of God, so they are not credible history. Others link the birth narratives with midrashes in Judaism which are religious commentaries about basic belief. They argue that the Christmas story evolved in Christian circles as a result of Christian discussion about the relationship between God and Christ. In this view the Christ of Faith has replaced the Jesus of history.

Some scholars have suggested that Jesus was born out of wedlock. His mother was deceived by a man who passed himself off as a messenger of God. Another theory was that Jesus was the fruit of an adulterous union between Mary and Panthera, a Roman soldier, as a result of which Mary was cast out of her home by her husband the carpenter.

In Jewish custom, betrothal was as binding as marriage, and the marriage was normally consummated after one year.

There is a barbed jibe in John chapter 8 verse 41, where the Pharisees say to Jesus 'We are not illegitimate children....the only Father we have is God Himself.' My New Testament tutor, Dr Donald Guthrie, a wonderful Christian and a world class scholar, commented on this verse 'it is possible that John 8 v 41 contains a sly allusion to rumours that Jesus' birth was irregular...' To Jews of the period, the idea of Virgin Birth brought God into degrading contact with the sinful world. To them it was abhorrent that God could take the place of a human father and beget children like the gods of the pagan world. This abhorrence would be intensified since during the period between the Old and New Testaments, Jewish theology had developed a more remote and transcendent view of God.

Finally, we may accept that miracles are possible, and this one is unique, second only to the Resurrection. If the Resurrection is possible, then no objection needs to be raised against the Christmas story of the Incarnation.

There are other parts of the New Testament which argue for the sinlessness of Jesus, so the Gospel writers did not have to invent stories. A literal view of the Christmas story fits perfectly with the general New Testament picture of Jesus as the Son of God who is also a perfect human being.

There's a Christian song which says:
> 'No room for the Baby in Bethlehem's inn, only a cattle shed,
> No place on this earth for the dear Son of God, Nowhere to lay His head;
> Only a Cross did they give to my Lord, only a borrowed tomb,
> Today He is seeking a place in your heart, will you still say to Him,' No room!'.

My hope and prayer for everyone who reads this is that you'll be able to join in the second verse:

'O Lord in my heart, there's a welcome for you, gladly I now would say,
Come in precious Saviour, my heart and my life both shall be yours today;
Long have You waited and long knocked in vain, outside my heart's closed door;
So cleanse me from sin, then, my Lord enter in, and live there for evermore!'

We are looking at Jesus the Miracle-maker, and particularly the narratives of His Birth in Matthew and Luke's Gospel. Nothing is known of Mary's home life before Jesus' birth. Some would think that since marriage could take place from mid-teens in Jewish custom at that time, Mary could be younger than we would imagine. Some scholars think that the four brothers and at least two sisters of Jesus mentioned in Mark chapter 6 were Joseph's children by a former marriage, so Joseph was therefore much older than Mary. It is futile to speculate, even though we enjoy it! We know it was the custom for the eldest son of a family to follow the father's trade, and we know that both Joseph and Jesus were carpenters, so the implication is that Jesus was the eldest son and the other family members came into the world after Jesus in the good old-fashioned way...Both Mary and Joseph had King David back in their genealogy.
Luke's Gospel tells the story from Mary's viewpoint: 'The Holy Spirit will come upon you, and the power of the Most High will overshadow you. So the holy one to be born will be called the Son of God.'

The language used is reminiscent of Genesis 1 verse 1 -2, where the Spirit of God brooded over an emerging creation like a bird over an incubating egg. This was of huge concern for Mary since her pregnancy would become apparent before the consummation of her marriage.

Matthew's Gospel tells the story from Joseph's viewpoint. He was in a delicate position to say the least. How could Mary expect Joseph to believe her story? He took it as a clear case of unfaithfulness, and immediately decided on divorce. In Jewish custom, this could take place publicly before a court or privately before two witnesses. Sensitive to Mary's feelings, Joseph chose the latter. He was a man of honour, responsive to God's leading, and accepted c revelation in a dream that the coming birth was supernaturally prepared.

Some scholars think the Gospel of Matthew was woven round a collection of Old Testament proof texts, like the quote from Isaiah 7 verse4 repeated in Matthew 1 verses 22,23 : 'All this took place to fulfil what the Lord had said through the prophet 'The virgin shall conceive and will give birth to a son, and they will call him Immanuel – which means 'God with us.' The Greek New Testament has the word 'parthenos' for 'virgin', and so has the Greek Old Testament, the Septuagint, which have this clear and unequivocal meaning, but the Old Testament Hebrew text uses the word 'almah' which is used of a young woman who may or may not be a virgin. If the Old Testament text had used 'bethulah' which is specifically 'a virgin', a lot of scholarly ink could have been spared! Donald Guthrie says 'Matthew clearly has in mind a pure young unmarried woman. Indeed, neither Matthew's or Luke's narrative conveys any suggestion that Mary the mother of Jesus was not a virgin.'

What does this mean to us, wherever we live, on a wet Wednesday?! Well it means that we have a record we can trust in the New Testament, and Saviour we can trust, in the Lord Jesus Christ. He is not some kind of Santa Claus figure, a man dressed up as God, but the fulfilment of hopes which were centuries old. Job, a rich sheikh who became a wretched sufferer said about the problem of reaching God: 'If only there were someone to arbitrate between us, to lay his hand upon us both' (JOB 9 v 33). Well the Christmas message is that there is a Mediator, and that Jesus has come to put us in vital contact with God. That was his mission on earth. The Baby of Bethlehem became the man of Calvary who died for our sins and rose to give us fresh hope in Him...

If you visit modern Israel, you would find a land flowing with potato crisps and Coca Cola instead of milk and honey! Anywhere that Jesus stopped for more than half an hour, it seems, they have put up a big building, like the Church of the Nativity in Bethlehem. Some parts of the country remain beautiful and unspoiled, especially in the Galilee area. In Judaea, I prefer to think that Jesus was born in one of the limestone caves on the hill of the shepherds outside Bethlehem, a rough and ready extension to living quarters, where the animals were kept. The manger was a feeding trough for animals, and Jesus' first visitors were the shepherds, according to Luke's account. Some have suggested they provided sheep for sacrifice at the Jerusalem Temple. They would be regarded by the religious leaders of the day as the 'am ha-arets', the people of the land, whose ceremonial defilement delayed Messiah's coming.

Then there were the men of science that Matthew writes about, the students of the stars, possibly from Mesopotamia, the flat land with the clear skies, who tracked SuperNova Bethlehem, or whatever else it was, and came to worship. The traditional view that there were three 'wise men' is based on their three gifts, and people have gone so far as to provide them with names. Jesus is worthy of worship right across the scale of social, financial, and any other kinds of power or achievement. Luke's account introduces us to the godly coterie, like Simeon and Anna, who were waiting and praying for 'the consolation of Israel'. Spare a prayer for our land, and for God's intervention, each Christmas, for there are dark forces pregnant with menace gathering around us. All around us are folks whose hearts are failing them for fear – fear of redundancy, terrorism, the incursions of exclusive groups before whom a supine government and a feeble church seem powerless.

What's in a name, or a nickname? As a schoolteacher, and as a metallurgist in the steelworks/ironworks, I moved in a busy world of people and their nicknames. At school, we had Prune and Fleabag and Sparrow, at work we had Cowboy, the Hangman and Dear Oh Dear Dawson (the Salvationist melter in the steelworks who said 'dear o dear' instead of swearing when the furnaces were acting up).

Let's finish this chapter about the Miracle of Christmas by reflecting on Jesus' name, and His nickname. In Matthew's version of the Christmas story, Joseph was told that Mary would give birth to a Son, and he was to give Him the name 'Jesus', for He will save His people from their sins. Jesus was a name of many facets, like a precious diamond. It is **a humble name**, grounded in poverty, in the backwater town called Nazareth, in the pigeons, the offering of the poor given by Mary and Joseph at His birth, in the patched clothing Jesus referred to in His teaching. It was a name shrouded in mystery in His hidden years of childhood, teenage and twenties. In His thirties when He was a travelling Rabbi, He announced the messianic secret of His mission of humiliation, death and resurrection to His disciples, and then ordered them to be silent about it. It was a humble name. It is also **a human name**, the Greek equivalent of the Hebrew Joshua, the Old Testament hero and successor to Moses. It was a name widely used, when disused through disgust or respect. Then it is **an honoured name,** in the memories it evokes of His limitless love demonstrated in His Cross and sufferings, in the message it contains of the hope of forgiveness and freedom for those who believe in Him, and in the miracles it still works in transformed individuals and changed families.

Jesus was given what was meant to be a cruel nickname which has become a badge of honour . The religious leaders of His time called Him 'The Friend of Sinners.' As a poor sinner saved by His grace, that gives me hope that He can be my Friend, and yours too!

There are three things we can do, faced by Jesus the Friend of Sinners.

'Though Christ a thousand times in Bethlehem be born,
If He's not born in you, your soul is all forlorn.'

Firstly, we should **believe** in this name, moving towards Him with a strong commitment. Secondly, we should **belong** to this name, and never be ashamed of confessing our loyalty to Him to other people. Thirdly, we should **bow down** to this name, and give Him our adoration and worship as long as we live.

QUESTIONS.

1. Which festival do you prefer – Christmas or Easter? Support your preferences.

2. Is Christmas a more important festival than Easter for Christians? Discuss.

3. Why do you think the Protestant Reformers did not want to observe Christmas a s a special festival?

4. Should we venerate the Virgin Mary? Discuss

5. What is your opinion of Joseph regarding Mary and the Birth of Jesus?

6. Are dreams and visions part of God's present-day revelation? Should we believe in angels? Discuss.

CHAPTER 17

VERSES TO MEMORISE.

In the absence of cheap writing materials, memorisation was a vital part of ancient learning.

In modern times, mind-training has an increasingly prominent role. In Christian education, the work of the Navigators has proved helpful in Christian service.

Here are some verses from our studies which could prove useful.
The Psalmist wrote: 'I have hidden Your word in my heart that I might not sin against You.'

Quotations are from the New International Version

CHAPTER 1   The Bible and the Parable

'All Scripture is God-breathed and is useful for teaching, rebuking, correcting and training in righteousness.'
2 Timothy chapter 3 verse 16.

CHAPTER 2   The Parable of the Sower

'But the one who received the seed that fell on good soil is the man who hears and understands it. He produces a crop, yielding a hundred, sixty or thirty times what was sown.'
Matthew chapter 13 verse 23.

CHAPTER 3   The Parable of the Prodigal Son

'So he got up and went to his father. But while he was still along way off, his father saw him and was filled with compassion for him; he ran to his son, threw his arms around him and kissed him.'
Luke chapter 15 verse 20.

CHAPTER 4   Rich and Foolish

'But God said to him, 'You fool! This very night your life will be demanded from you. Then who will get what you have prepared for yourself? This is how it will be with anyone who stores up things for himself but is not rich towards God.' Luke chapter 12 verses 20 and 21.

CHAPTER 5   Two Prayer Parables

'But the tax collector stood at a distance. He would not even look up to heaven but beat his breast and said, 'God have mercy on me, a sinner.'
Luke chapter 18 verse 13.

CHAPTER 6   Rich Man, Poor Man

'He said to him, 'If they do not listen to Moses and the Prophets, they will not be convinced even if someone rises from the dead.'
Luke chapter 16 verse 31.

CHAPTER 7   The Crooked Manager

'No man can serve two masters. Either he will hate the one and love the other, or he will be devoted to the one and despise the other. You cannot serve God and money.'
Luke chapter 16 verse 13.

CHAPTER 8   The Corrupt Farmhands

Jesus looked directly at them and asked, Then what is the meaning of that which is written: 'The stone the builders rejected has become the capstone' Everyone who falls on that stone will be broken to pieces, but he on whom it falls will be crushed.
Luke chapter 20 verses 17-18.

CHAPTER 9   What is a Miracle?

'But if I drive out demons by the finger of God, then the kingdom of God has come to you.'
Luke chapter 11 verse 20.

CHAPTER 10   A Paralytic Walks

'But that you may know that the Son of Man has authority on earth to forgive sins...He said to the paralytic, 'I tell you, get up, take up your mat, and go home.'
Mark chapter 2 verses 10-11

CHAPTER 11   The Man at the Pool

'Later Jesus found him and said to him, 'See, you are well again. Stop sinning, or something worse may happen to you.'
John chapter 5 verse 14.

CHAPTER 12   The Crowd on the Hill

'Then Jesus declared, 'I am the bread of life. He who comes to me will never go hungry, and he who believes in me will never be thirsty.'

CHAPTER 13   Jesus Spoils a Funeral Party

'They were all filled with awe and praised God. 'A great prophet has appeared among us,' they said. 'God has come to help His people.'
John chapter 7 verse 16.

CHAPTER 14   The Deaf Man from Decapolis

People were overwhelmed with amazement. 'He has done everything well,' they said. 'He even makes the deaf hear and the mute speak.'
Mark chapter 7 verse 37

CHAPTER 15   The Madman and the Pigs

'When they came to Jesus, they found the man from whom the demons had gone out, sitting at Jesus' feet, dressed and in his right mind; and they were afraid.'
Luke chapter 8 verse 35.

CHAPTER 16   The Miracle of Christmas

'An angel of the Lord appeared to him in a dream, saying, 'Joseph son of David, do not be afraid to take Mary home as your wife, because what is conceived in her is from the Holy Spirit. She will give birth to a son, and you are to give Him the name Jesus, because He will save His people from their sins.'
Matthew chapter 1 verses 20-21.